Fast

MW00913208

Create Video CD's

M.-S. Goewecke

DATA BECKER®

Contents

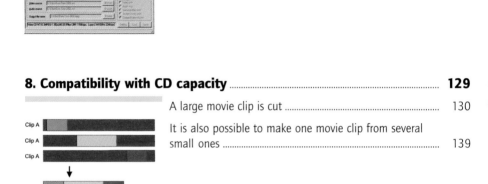

From tape to disc

Only 20 years ago, the amateur film enthusiast captured his home environment on Super 8 film. This was almost completely replaced in the 90s by video taping. Within this new medium, a further transformation occurred in the last few years: camcorders have become increasingly digital and have in the meantime made it possible to capture videos with cameras handy enough to fit in a handbag while retaining a quality that almost rivals that of a professional TV camera.

Thanks to the digital age, video and computer technology has in the meantime converged so much that, in the ideal scenario – when using digital video formats such as miniDV or Digital8 – there is no more conversion (digitalization) necessary. A video's data stream only has to be copied to the hard drive, where it can be edited in any imaginable way.

The VHS cassette is threatened with becoming extinct in a few years. It is already being replaced by DVDs, the "CD for movies".

Anyone who is of the opinion that such players can only play back prefabricated DVDs or DVDs created with what are still extremely expensive burners is wrong, for almost every DVD player has the capability to play back video CDs (VCDs).

All that's needed is a computer with a CD burner and a couple of software tools, and already a video playable on a DVD player can be put forth.

With a quality similar to that of a VHS cassette, up to 80 minutes of video can be recorded on a video CD using commercially available blank CDs (CD-Rs).

Movie makers can, for example, copy entire tapes to CD and use these for viewing purposes.

Your children's cartoons can also be saved to video CDs instead of to VHS. Fast forwarding and rewinding the tape isn't necessary, and using the CD is a piece of cake.

One step higher: the Super video CD

In addition to the video CD, you can also find an even higher resolution Super video CD (SVCD), which is covered in more detail in the "From VHS to DVD", incidentally also published by DATA BECKER.

1. VirtualDub: the free capturing program

Windows itself offers an internal method of importing video data only since Windows XP. However, Movie Maker is quite a bare-bones program. If you have an older Windows version or are looking for farther-reaching editing possibilities, it is recommended you look for further software.

If you are afraid that the purchase of another program is now in order, you can calm down.

A particularly large selection of video editing software tools is available free of charge (i.e. as freeware). One of these freeware tools is VirtualDub.

VirtualDub on the WWW

The easiest way to acquire VirtualDub is through the Internet. In addition to the newest current verision of the program, useful information and links can be found on the author's website.

http://www.virtualdub.org

VirtualDub has in the meantime become a classic. It is used for the capturing of video images and offers a variety of very useful functions.

VirtualDub makes it possible, for example, to circumvent the restrictive size limitations placed on video files by simply dividing the video stream into several blocks of a definable size. This way, the seamless recording of 30 GBs of material over two 20 GB drives is no problem.

Technical requirements for capturing

In order to be able to capture video with the computer, your equipment needs to meet certain minimal requirements.

1. VirtualDub: the free capturing program

A program such as VirtualDub is naturally dependent on a video card which is based on Video for Windows.

There are the following possibilities:

Graphics cards with video input

In many cases, an additional card is not necessary, if the computer's graphics card already comes with such inputs.

If there are one or more connections next to the connector for the monitor (with descriptions such as "AV-in", "Video-in", "Video Line-in", or "S-Video in"), then everything is looking good, for you can most likely avoid purchasing an additional video card.

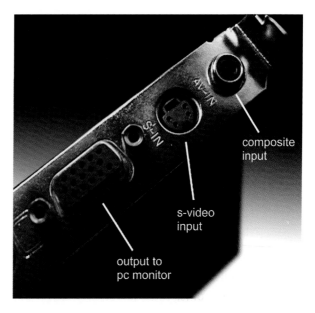

composite input

s-video input

output to pc monitor

However, the video card is solely responsible for the picture – a sound card is absolutely necessary, but does not involve any large investment these days.

The entire connection will then look somewhat like the one in the illustration.

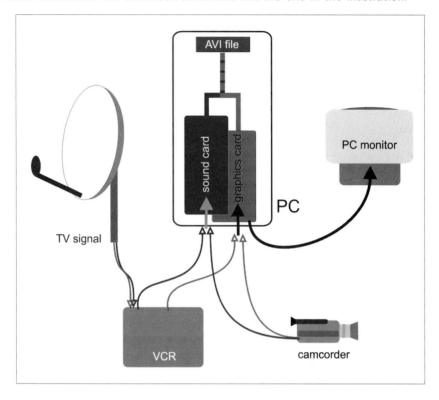

TV cards

If your graphics card doesn't feature a video input, you can purchase a television card, which standardly possesses such a connection.

This card, with TV tuner, makes the reception of television programs and the transmission from other video sources possible over the said inputs, assuming you have a satellite dish/cable/satellite connection.

1. VirtualDub: the free capturing program

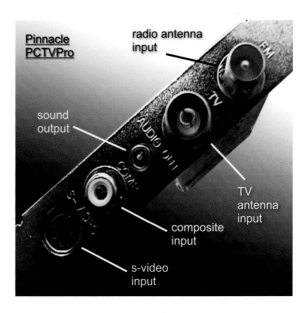

Depending on the equipment, an additional sound card may also be necessary here, so that the sound can be recorded as well.

A strong advantage of this arrangement is that the received TV programs can be recorded to the hard drive and made into video CDs.

Are TV cards with MPEG capturing better for (Super) video CDs?

Newer TV cards already capture in MPEG-2 format. The video image retains the same quality but is "packed" much tighter, therefore using less space and reducing the dependency on the hard drive's speed.

If you think you only have to burn these files to CD in order to create a SVCD you've got it wrong. Even here, a conversion using some software is necessary, for the MPEG-2 format for a SVCD has to contain very specific parameters.

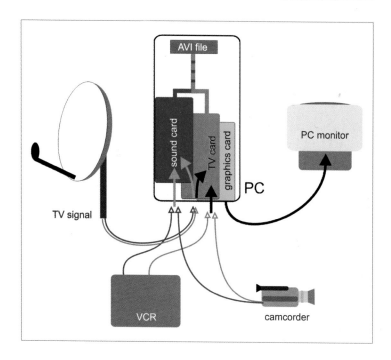

Video capture cards

Another option for video input is a video capture card with analog inputs.

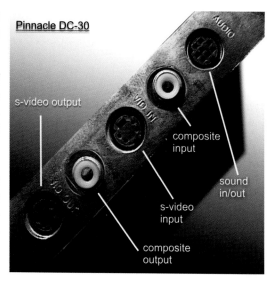

Such cards offer a wide range of features and cost approximately $100. However, you can also easily spend a couple of thousand dollars on one.

For those who primarily want to capture their own video images and burn them onto CDs, a special video capture board is probably the best solution.

1. VirtualDub: the free capturing program

You don't even have to sacrifice TV capturing. To record TV images, you can tap into the signal through most video recorder output channels.

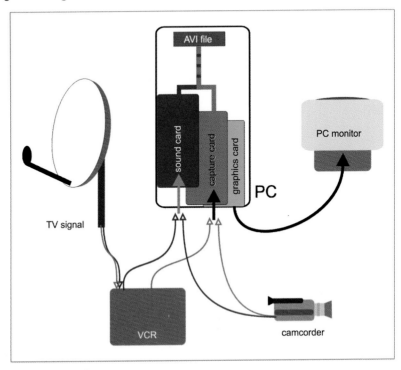

FireWire cards

In the meantime, the Mini-DV format has become the standard for consumer camcorders. If you wish to transfer your self-made movies to your computer, you will need a so-called FireWire card (also known as i-link or IEEE-1394); the basic card starts at around $80. With this card, the already digitized data contained on the cassette (digitized by the camera during recording) only needs to be copied to the hard drive.

A television picture can be reproduced in two ways with this card: If the camcorder uses an analog input for the video signal, the TV signal can be fed through the camcorder from a VCR. It will then be in digital format at the DV output of the camera, from where it can be transferred to the computer. The camcorder acts as an analog-to-digital converter.

Even more convenient, and with optimal picture quality, is the use of a VCR with a FireWire connection, which are present on the DV/SVHS combination devices from JVC, for example.

VirtualDub and FireWire

The creators of VirtualDub are already working on support for FireWire cards, so that this feature can be counted on appearing within the next few versions. Generally, most editing programs, including freeware tools such as MovieXone, master DV recording.

Faster, bigger: the hard drives

Video files need a lot of space.

Even with compression processes, recording an hour of good-quality video may take up to 10 GB.

Thanks to modern transfer standards like UDMA-100, inexpensive IDE drives can also cope with the data stream.

Install the drivers carefully!

It is always advised to optimize the performance of the hard drive by installing the bus master driver for the mainboard, which provides for a constant data transfer between the components (in this case, the graphics/TV or video cards).

If your PC has been used previously only for Office applications, you will become aware of the system weaknesses and driver problems during such demanding activities as recording videos.

1. VirtualDub: the free capturing program

Installing VirtualDub

VirtualDub does not have a setup routine like most other programs.

You simply have to copy the directory to a desired position, usually in the default folder *Programs*.

Determining the speed of the hard drive

For video capture with PCs, the speed of the hard drive is of the essence, as it determines the quality of the captured images. The so-called data transfer rate is also important here, for it informs you how many files per second can be written. The higher the number, the faster the drive.

With the help of an additional program, VirtualDub can test the performance of the hard drive and determine the data transfer rate.

The AuxSetup program can be found in the VirtualDub directory and principally offers two ways of determining the performance of the hard drive, whereby the second variant yields more practical and comprehensive results in the *Peak disk performance* field.

In this variant, the hard drive's average data thruput is determined by means of first writing and then reading a test file. The time required for completing this process provides information about the speed.

1 After starting the Setup tool, the following window will appear, in which you can gain access to the *Disk performance test* by clicking the *Benchmark* button.

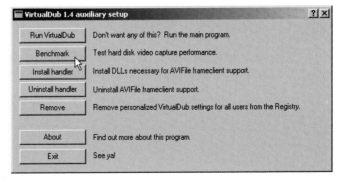

The subsequent dialog box can determine the performance properties of the relevant hard drive.

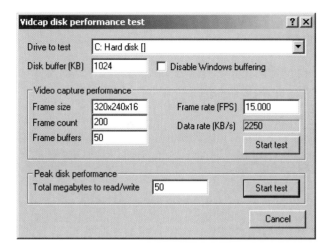

2 Select the relevant drive.

3 Now you only need to indicate the size of the test file – and then you can proceed.

Here, too, the bigger the test file, the more reliable the result. With such a result, there should be no problems with capturing. It is advised not to think of this value as the definitive one, as test procedures lasting a relatively short time can only provide approximate results.

1. VirtualDub: the free capturing program

Keep your settings below the values obtained in order to avoid as much image loss as possible.

Which way to the recording?

Double-clicking on *VirtualDub.exe* launches the program and this start screen – the part of the program where video clips can be edited, shortened, converted, or filtered.

The "recording studio" hides behind the *File/Capture AVI...* menu item.

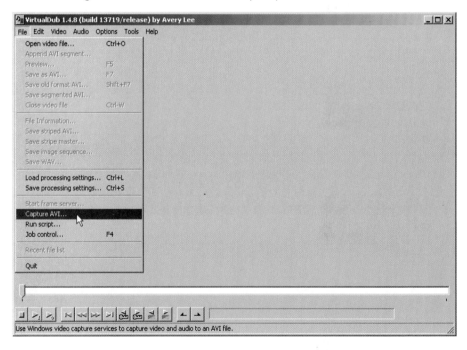

In order for VirtualDub to "find" the video image in your PC and record it, the hardware that is providing the image must be compatible with Video for Windows and have the relevant drivers installed.

Some cards have their own, incompatible drivers, but most are (semi) professional interface cards, like Matrox RT2000, which use their own capturing tool.

If VirtualDub has no drivers available which are compatible with Video for Windows, a warning message will appear.

If your hardware should have such drivers, according to the manufacturer's information, then read the relevant manuals and install the hardware anew, if necessary.

If there were no problems, the capturing window of VirtualDub will appear.

Only a blue/green screen instead of an image?

Ideally, the video signal inputted by you should then appear in the window, be it the image from a TV card, a video recorder, or a connected camcorder.

It is not as good if instead only a blue or green window appears.

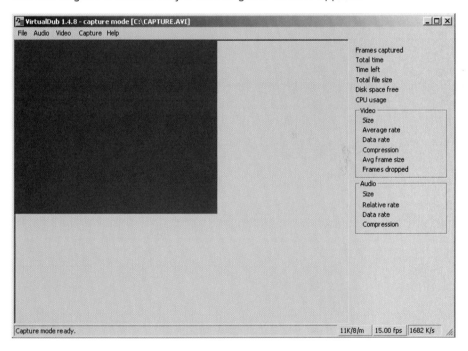

Still, no need to worry: the signs are good. Usually, a blue screen is displayed if a capturing driver but no image has been found.

1. VirtualDub: the free capturing program

When the program is first started, it is generally necessary to tweak a few basic settings to determine how something is to be recorded and to where.

Usually, this procedure will also uncover the causes for the lack of an image.

VirtualDub's default settings

Before capturing can begin, a few settings have to be tweaked in the program. You can save these settings, so that you only have to do this once.

Determining the capture disk or file

VirtualDub can determine the capturing drive and directory, so that different projects will not get mixed up.

1 Select *File/Set capture file...*

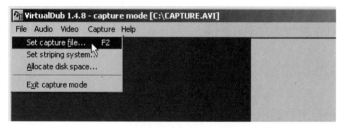

2 After selecting the drive and the directory you can then leave the file selection dialog box.

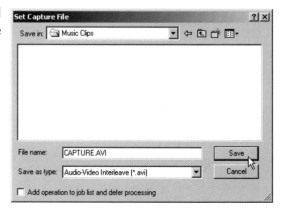

Avoid using the OS drive!

If at all possible, you should not record on the default drive C, as this is where Windows usually saves its temporary files. Ideally, a second hard drive would be used exclusively to save video files.

Video and audio settings

Both the video and the audio files should be compressed when captured, in order to reduce the huge amounts of data that are involved to a more manageable size.

Selecting the sound format

1 Go to *Audio/Compression*.

2 A dialog window for selecting the audio compression appears.

3 Here, we select ADPCM compression.

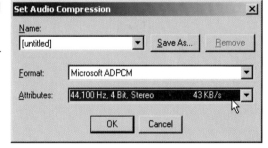

ADPCM

Compared to the standard PCM format, which is also used for audio CDs (44,1KHz, 16 Bit, Stereo), the compressed ADPCM variant uses only a quarter of the space (43 KB/s instead of 172 KB/s) with very little loss in quality.

23

1. VirtualDub: the free capturing program

Regulating the sound

VirtualDub has a built-in module for displaying the sound level of the currently set volume level.

1 Go to *Audio/Volume meter.*

2 Move the volume sliders until the sound level indicators representing the highest level of the sound that is do be recorded are shortly before the right limit.

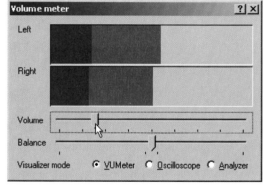

If a mono sound is selected under *Audio/Compression...* , only one channel is displayed.

> **Better too loud than too quiet**
> It's not recommended to move the level all the way to the end because peaking will quickly lead to noticeable distortion. If in doubt, rather choose a somewhat lower level.

Selecting the video source

Now, we want to make the pesky blue window disappear. The blue window usually means that the Video-in has not been selected correctly.

The menu option *Video/Source...* will take care of this.

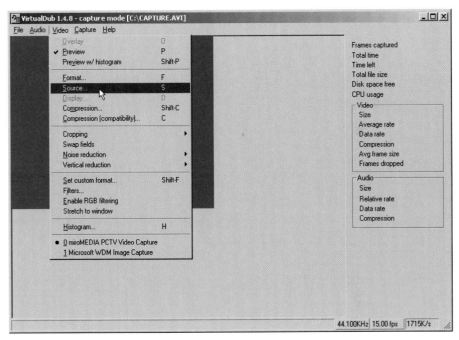

The TV card used here (Pinnacle PCTV Pro) was set to *Composite* (Line-in), and, as no device was connected there, the blue screen appeared.

TV cards and Windows XP

Make sure that you have the most current version of your driver installed under Windows XP. In case of problems, always refer back to the manufacturer's website for possible solutions. The problem arises because Windows XP basically supports only WDM drivers, and, at least at the time this book was produced, they were not completely developed. Alternatively, you could also try to install the Windows 2000 drivers.

1. VirtualDub: the free capturing program

Clicking on *Tuner* connects the TV signal of the receiver to the card, which appears immediately in the main window.

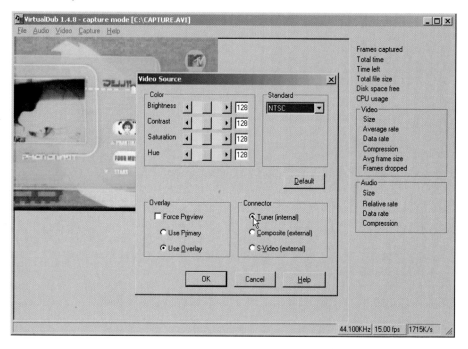

Features like type and number of Video-ins or the image parameters available can also be found here.

The available settings within the dialog area depend completely on the hardware you are using; therefore, the following dialog areas can vary signifcantly in their functionality and appeerence.

The individual areas:

Setting the color, contrast, and color saturation

With the three sliders, you can set the *Brightness, Contrast* and *Saturation* for the active Video-in.

The adjustments are shown in real time in the main window.

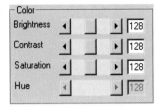

Selecting the TV standard

Here, you must select the TV standard used. In Germany, the standard is PAL, in France, for example, SECAM, and in the USA we use NTSC.

Setting the overlay

By "Overlay" we mean the way the video image is shown on the computer monitor.

This "foreign" signal can be integrated ("overlaid") into the current image in different ways, depending on the capabilities of the PC's graphics card.

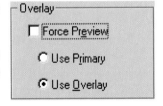

With this card, there are three modes available. If you use the *Use Overlay* option, the graphics card will primarily concern itself with reproducing the video image, assuming it supports this function. For the video capturing, this spells some relief for the main processor, which can then fully and completely dedicate itself to the compression of the video image.

1. VirtualDub: the free capturing program

Should there be problems with displaying the video image on the computer monitor, adjustments could prove helpful. If your driver does not support overlay settings, you can only use the corresponding VirtualDub menu option, *Video/Overlay*. With serious problems, you can go back to the uncomplicated (choppy) Preview mode (*Video/Preview*).

Choosing the signal in

This TV card has two other Video-in options in addition to the actual tuner to which you can connect a video recorder or camcorder.

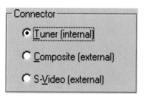

Should the device have an S-video-out and – as here – a corresponding in channel, you should select the composite signal, because the image quality is visibly better due to the separate transfer of brightness and color values.

Selecting the video format

The format of the video to be captured should be selected with care, as it determines the quality and the space used by the file created.

The video format incorporates three parameters. They are:

• The pixel measurements of the image.

• The image format (colorspace).

• The compression format.

The following settings can vary in terms of content and form depending on the TV card used. A Pnnacle PCTV Pro card was used here.

1 You can reach the settings by going to *Video/Format.*

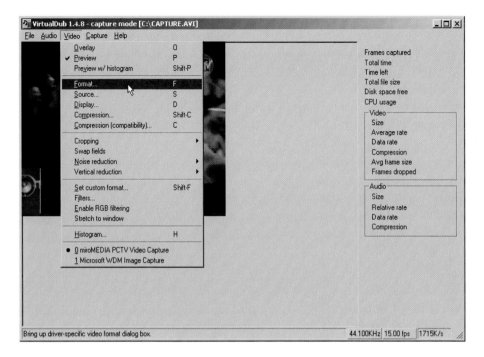

Here, you can also find the options provided by the hardware drivers.

2 Under *Image Dimensions,* you can determine the image resolution.

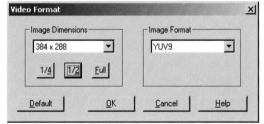

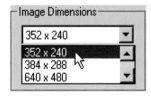

If you want to create a standard video CD from the material captured, you must set the corresponding resolution, namely 352x240 pixels – a format that can be handled even by the "small" cards. Thus, you see how a video CD can be created without using complex hardware.

1. VirtualDub: the free capturing program

The default setting of PCTV Pro is a frame size of 384x240 pixels. To spare the MPEG encoder the trouble of converting the horizontal resolution from 384 to 352 later (which can lead to image deterioration), the video CD should be recorded in the latter resolution.

3 In addition, the color space (or color model) has to be set.

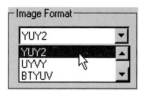

The quality and size of the data depend on how the analog TV image was scanned during digitalization.

The relevant image formats can be found in the list field and are usually described in the graphics, TV or video card manual.

In our example, the setting *YUV2* provides the best quality.

4 To set up the video compression, go to *Video/Compression*.

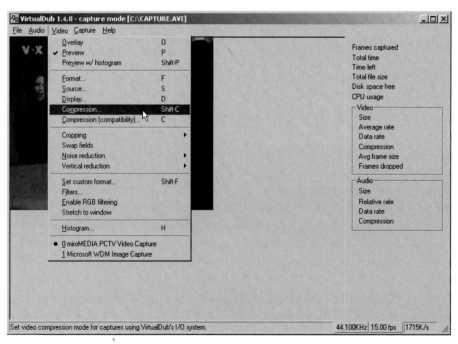

In the selection window that then appears, a list of available codecs for the relevant driver is displayed.

Select the codec. (In this example, the Indeo codec has been selected because it is best suited for capturing with this card.)

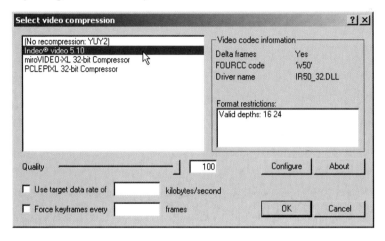

Compressors

Similarly, you need to select so-called compressors – in essence, small programs containing encryption instructions – for both the image and the sound components of the video.

Such "instructions" are also named *codecs* (from **co**ding/**de**coding) and are either integrated into the hardware so that they can be executed by special processors (hardware codecs) or small software modules that can be installed on the system (software codecs).

Again: this is not a complete list of codecs installed on the system, but simply a selection of those with which capturing is possible.

With the slider found below, you can select the configuration quality of the codec.

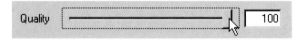

1. VirtualDub: the free capturing program

The farther to the right you set the slider, the better the image quality and the higher the data transfer rate.

Depending on the purpose of your VCD, it is advised that test capturing be carried out with different settings to get a feel for the quality to be expected from different positions on the slide bar.

More "settings" before the first recording

Now, all should be prepared for the first recording.

In the bottom right corner of the capture window of VirtualDub, you can find the Quick Menu, in which the most important parameters can be viewed.

You can see here that the frame rate is 15 fps  (frames per second); thus, the number of images to be recorded per second does not correspond to the frame rate of our TV system (29.97 fps).

Note

Frame rates

There are two frame rates for TV signals worldwide: 25 frames per second with PAL (e.g. in Germany) and SECAM (e. g. in France), and 29.97 frames per second with NTSC (e. g. in the US).

With this Quick Menu, you can change the values by clicking with the mouse.

You can adjust the frame rate settings as follows:

1 Click on the frame rate button.

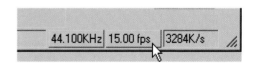

2 A table opens, from which *29.97* fps is selected.

Integral	NTSC	Nearest ms
60.00 fps	59.94 fps	30.30 fps
30.00 fps	29.97 fps	29.41 fps
25.00 fps	19.98 fps	15.15 fps
20.00 fps	14.99 fps	14.93 fps
15.00 fps	11.99 fps	
12.00 fps	9.99 fps	
10.00 fps		
5.00 fps		

And more settings ...

With respect to the capturing process, still more settings can be made:

1 Go to *Capture/Settings.*

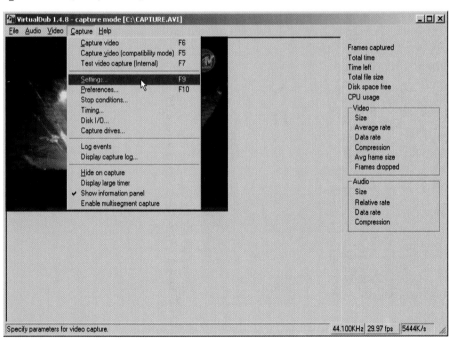

1. VirtualDub: the free capturing program

2 A dialog window containing all the parameters opens.

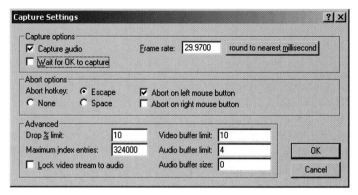

3 If sound is going to be recorded, *Capture audio* must be selected.

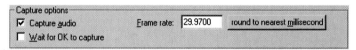

4 The *Wait for OK to capture* option introduces a window that you must confirm when you start capturing.

5 The *Frame rate* changed previously in the Quick menu can also be changed numerically here.

6 In the *Abort options* area at the bottom, you can determine which (mouse) button can abort the capture. In this example, using the (Esc) key or right-clicking will lead to aborting the capture process.

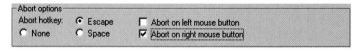

The *Advanced* options should be left alone.

VirtualDub saves your settings

Obviously, you do not have to make these settings again every time you start the program ...

The achieved state can be saved as the default to be used every time the program starts.

1 To save it, go to *Capture/Preferences.*

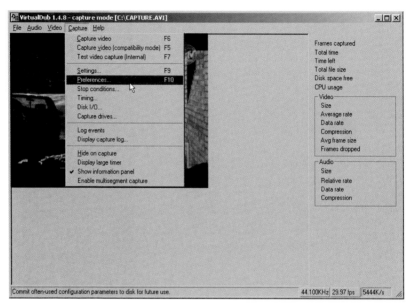

2 In the corresponding region in the window, enable all the *Save* options.

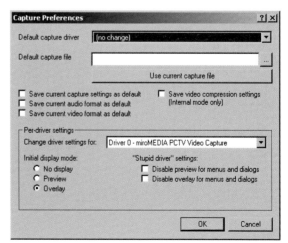

☑ Save current capture settings as default	☑ Save video compression settings
☑ Save current audio format as default	(Internal mode only)
☑ Save current video format as default	

Done.

Capturing in VirtualDub

Now we can really start the fun.

We want to record a music video from TV.

> **VirtualDub supports two recording modes**
>
> The compatibility mode leaves the actual recording to the system's own Video for Windows and ensures that the recording functions with most capture cards.
>
> When using the internal capture mode, VirtualDub takes care of all the capturing. One of the advantages is that it can create an adaptive data transfer rate, meaning that the data transfer rate is suited to the image content. This saves space.

Both modes are used regularly and appear twice in the menus. The compatibility mode is indicated by *(compatibility)* or *(compatibility mode)*:

The compression can be selected separately for each mode.

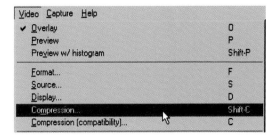

You can select the mode even when capturing.

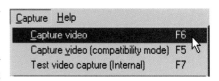

For the following capture procedure, the internal capture mode is used. If problems should arise, e.g. if images are lost during capture, the compatibility mode can always be used.

Attention, capturing!

Start capturing by going to *Capture/Capture video*. Alternatively, you can press F6.

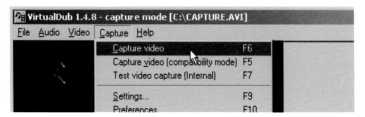

Information, information, information ...

During capturing, VirtualDub keeps you up-to-date by displaying a wealth of data on the right side of the capturing screen.

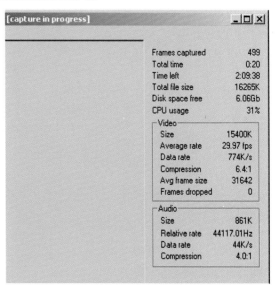

1. VirtualDub: the free capturing program

The following values are particularly interesting:

- *Time left*, just like *Disk space free, shows* the space still available on the relevant drive. The display in hours, minutes and seconds is much more descriptive.

- In the *Video* category, the data transfer rate is constantly displayed. If capturing in the compatibility mode, the number does not change, because you are working with a fixed data transfer rate. In the internal capture mode, you can see how the data transfer rate is made suitable to the complexity of the image.

- Also in the *Video category,* you can find *Frames dropped* which counts the frames that have not been captured in the drive, thus causing inconsistencies in the recorded video.

- In such a case, changes must be made to the video and audio settings. The root of the problem can be a data transfer rate that was set too high or a slow or poorly configured hard drive.

And ... cut!

Capturing can be aborted as determined in the capture settings.

Afterwards, you can see the live image as before.

New capture, new file!

Now you must pay attention!

If another capturing procedure has been started, VirtualDub then overwrites the clip just saved, as the clip is always captured under the file defined in *File/Set capture file.*

The following method is tried and true:

1 The capturing directory is displayed as a window next to VirtualDub.

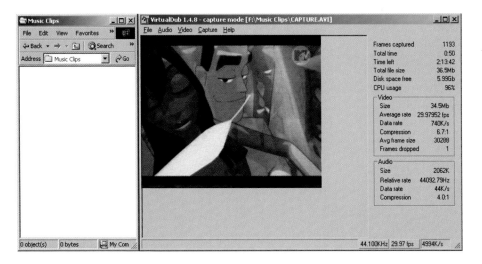

2 Go to *File/Set capture file*, and select the file *capture.avi* as the capture file.

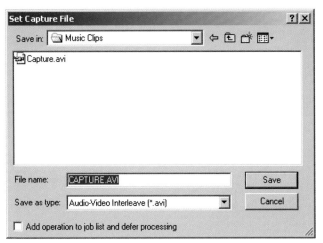

3 After the first clip has been recorded, *Capture.avi* appears in the neighboring window, and you can change its name.

4 Now you can resume capturing. After each capture, a *capture.avi* is created. Rename it, etc.

If it takes longer: AVI files bigger than 2 or 4 GB

If only short music videos were to be captured onto disk, as in the previous example, there would be no problem.

With an average data transfer rate of 700-1000 KB per second, the gravity of the situation only becomes apparent after 20 minutes: the resulting AVI file reaches 2 GB.

2 GB - a problem ...

Video for Windows has limited its hard drive partitions to 2 GB, which is also the maximum file size achievable for AVI files, since its introduction.

By extending the file system from FAT16 to FAT32, the limit for these files increases from 2 to 4 GB (the partitions can become even larger). The latest version of Windows 95 (OSR 2) and Windows 98 support the FAT32 file system. The AVI format itself still contained restrictions which could only be lifted with the advancement of the OpenDML standard.

Using the NTFS system will soon be a matter of course

Such file size problems will soon be a thing of the past, for, with the recent appearance of Windows XP, the Windows NT developed platform (New Technology File System) will finally be a household item. It makes extremely large file sizes possible (approx. 18,000 GB) and will be gladly taken up by people who work a lot with videos.

... and the solution

VirtualDub can facilitate capturing long segments even with Windows 95 - provided there is enough hard disk space - thanks to its *Multisegment capturing*.

The principle is simple to imagine:

Once the capture file reaches a certain size (which is freely defined), it is then closed very quickly and a new one is opened. If no more space is available in the hard drive or partition, VirtualDub can change to the next one.

Only a few settings are necessary to effectively handle the file size limit:

Defining the capturing drive

Imagine your PC has two hard drives:

On the first drive, there are partitions C and E, whereby the system is contained on C as usual. Partition E is for general data storage.

1. VirtualDub: the free capturing program

Another, faster drive is divided into partitions D and F, and is supposed to be used primarily for storing videos.

1 Under *Capture*, select the menu command *Capture drives*.

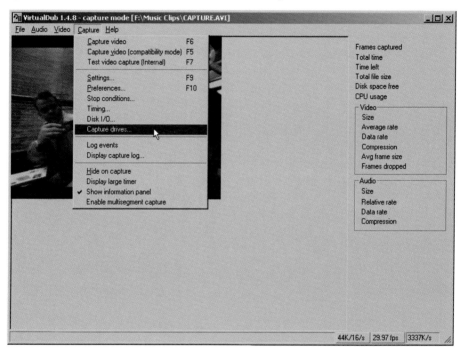

All necessary settings can be adjusted in the dialog box *Spill System Setup*:

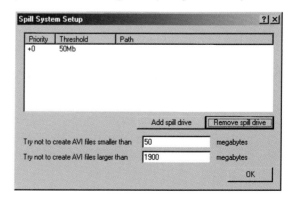

2 In the dialog window, click on *Path* and enter the path to the desired directory in which the clips are to be written.

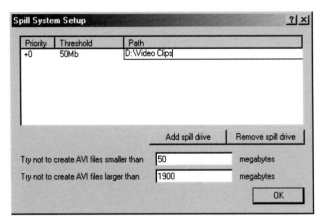

3 With the *Add spill drive* button you can add drives.

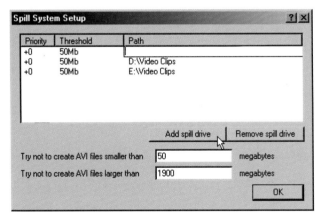

Partitions D and F should take priority, as they are on the fast drive, while E should only be used in an emergency.

Under *Priority*, you can rank the capture drives. The higher the number, the more likely that it will be used for capturing.

1. VirtualDub: the free capturing program

If two drives have the same value, the drive with the most free space is the first choice.

4 The priority for E should be set to 1 with the mouse, meaning that this partition is to be used only when the two faster drives are completely full.

5 In the bottom entry field of the dialog window, the maximum size of the video file is determined. The 1900 MB entered here ensure that a new file is created before the old one exceeds the 2 GB limit.

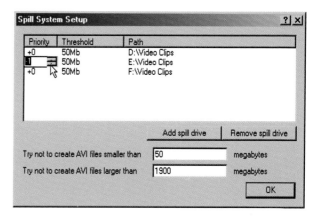

The value in *Threshold* determines at which amount of remaining space the drive should be changed. This value can be increased up to 127 MB.

With the *Remove spill drive* button, a defined and selected drive can be removed at a click of the mouse.

Finally, you can set the limit values for the files to be created in the entry fields at the bottom. The first parameter is the threshold value, which ensures that files below a certain size are not created.

Important: The standard file must now be placed on one of the fast drives in an appropriate directory.

You can select the appropriate directory quickly by going to *File/Set capture file.*

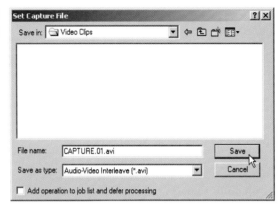

Enabling the spill system

After you have closed the dialog box, the defined spill system must be enabled.

This is done by checking the menu option *Capture/Enable multisegment capture.*

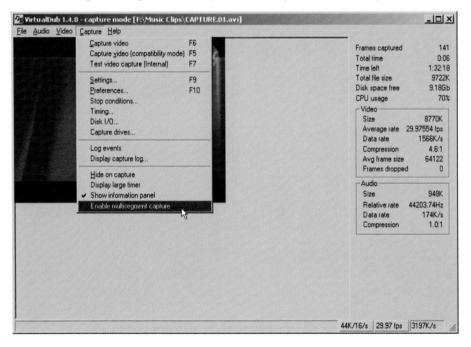

1. VirtualDub: the free capturing program

Important! Such multisegment capturing only functions when using the internal capture mode (*Capture/Capture video*)!

The compatibility mode does not support this feature, because such functions have not been integrated into Video for Windows.

The files created are assigned a number according to the following sequence and are handled like one file by VirtualDub:

- clipname.00.avi
- clipname.01.avi
- clipname.02.avi

...

In editing programs, these AVI blocks can be arranged in sequence so as to recreate the original movie.

To minimize possible problems, it is advised not to carry out audio compression during capture but to use the PCM or ADPCM format instead.

No space – what then?

After successful capturing, the capture drive may well be full.

If a data transfer rate of a mere 800 KB per second was used, a 90-minute long movie will take up to 4.3 GB.

If you want to burn this onto CDs, you will need 6 to 7 blank CDs and will have to change discs every 15 minutes – not very convenient ...

Now we can use VirtualDub's ability as a data converter, because choosing the definitive format is only limited by the number of codecs installed.

Find the best compression procedures for the image and sound. VirtualDub can then create finished AVI files. Here, image and sound can be interwoven or saved as separate files.

Codecs – where can you find them?

A codec is an "instruction" about how to code video or sound files so that they use less space. Usually, it also includes how to make a video movie out of an encrypted data stream (decoding).

We have already used such codecs for the video capture (see page 15), its most important role being to compress the video stream in real time.

Now, after the video has been saved on the drive, all of the other steps are not time-critical, meaning that even a codec that requires more computation time, but also leads to better results can now be used.

Windows has some of its own codecs, like Indeo or Cinepak, already installed. In our example, we will use Indeo for the clip we just captured.

Other formats, like Apple Quicktime which comes with many codecs, can be acquired separately or are parts of other software products, like video editing programs.

Additional hardware like TV or interface cards can install their own codecs on your system, which can then normally be used by programs like VirtualDub.

Shrinking movies after capturing

The captured music clip should now be converted to the common and Windows-compatible Indeo format.

MPEG-4 and DivX

New codecs such as MPEG-4 and DivX are becoming ever more popular because they allow for an even higher compression of the image. More detailed information about this topic can be found in the DATA BECKER line of books.

All necessary steps are carried out in the video processing mode, the "starting point" of VirtualDub.

1. VirtualDub: the free capturing program

1 If video clips have just been digitized, the capture mode can be changed by going to *File/Exit capture mode.*

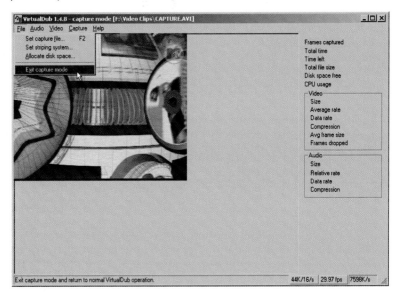

2 Go to *File/Open video file* to load the clip to be processed.

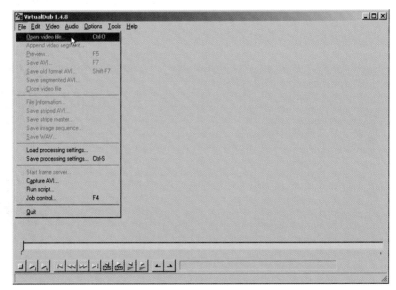

If two empty frames appear at first, move the slider below to display the video.

The image on the left side always shows the original, while the right shows the results of the process used, so you can assess the results.

Defining the starting and ending points

In the processing window, you have the option of marking the video clip, thereby defining new starting and ending points.

If you want to digitize music videos from television, as in the example, start capturing from the introduction and keep capturing until after the end of the clip.

Subsequent editing to the right length can then be carried out in VirtualDub:

1. VirtualDub: the free capturing program

1 Move towards the future starting point. With the slider, you can control the relevant position at least roughly.

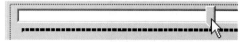

2 To locate the exact position of the very first image of the music video, use the relevant buttons.

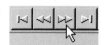

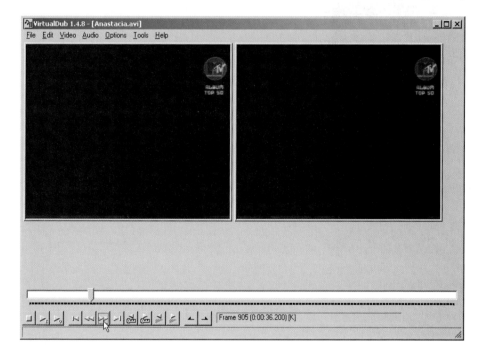

3 This position can then be marked with the In-Point button.

4 The ending point is marked in the same way. The marked area appears in blue.

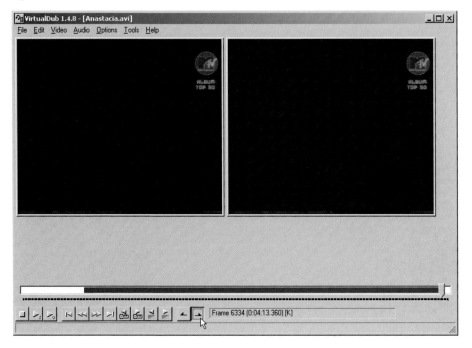

Processing mode and codec selection

After you have determined which sections are to be exported to the exact frame, you must select the codecs (the selection occurs separately for image and sound).

Setting the processing mode

The prospective video should only differ from the original in space needed, meaning that each individual frame should be decompressed in an RGB frame before being reduced further with a new codec. In order for VirtualDub to really do this, enable the *Full processing* mode menu option in the *Video menu*. With *Direct stream copy*, the video files would be copied unchanged without incorporating the parameters set.

1. VirtualDub: the free capturing program

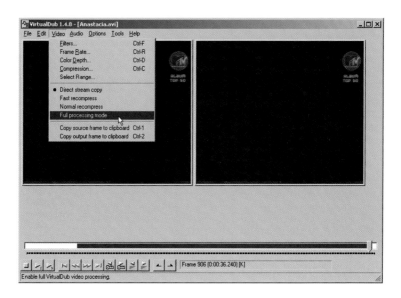

Under *Audio*, the *Full processing mode* must also be set.

Selecting the video codec

1 Go to *Video/Compression.*

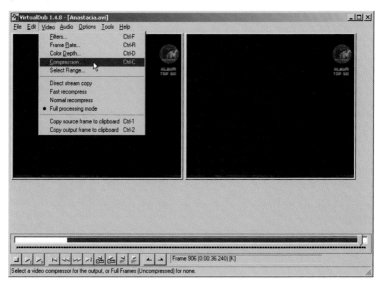

The list field shows all available codecs.

2 Select the desired output codec. In the *Format restrictions* window, all applicable restrictions you must consider are shown.

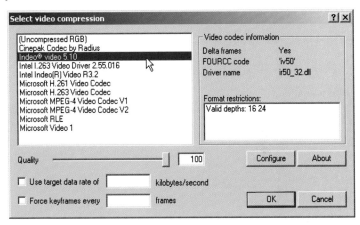

Click the *Configure* button to adjust specific settings for each codec.

3 The desired data transfer rate can be set numerically or with the slider.

The higher the value, the better the picture quality will be and the larger the resulting file.

4 Codecs such as Indeo are based on keyframes. In the corresponding entry field, a value needs to be entered to determine at what interval they should be set. Here, each 15th image should become the "key image" and the pre-image for the 14 images that follow.

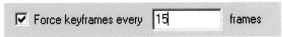

1. VirtualDub: the free capturing program

It is recommended to use one and the same video segment with different settings in order to learn about the strong and weak points of the codec.

We will leave this dialog window now and go back to VirtualDub's user interface so we can select the audio codec.

Selecting the audio codec

1 Here, select the menu option *Compression.*

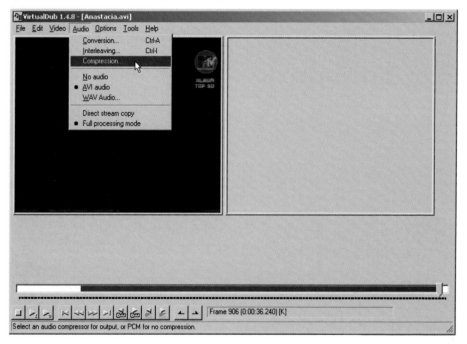

2 We will select the MPEG-3 codec here, because it is suitable for compressing not only pure sound files to a compact size, but also sound contained in a video clip.

3 In the window to the right, all of the available data rates are shown, from which we will select *96 kBit, 44,100 Hz stereo.*

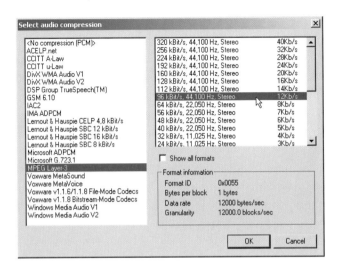

Saving the new video

The resulting video is created simply by going to *File/Save AVI:*

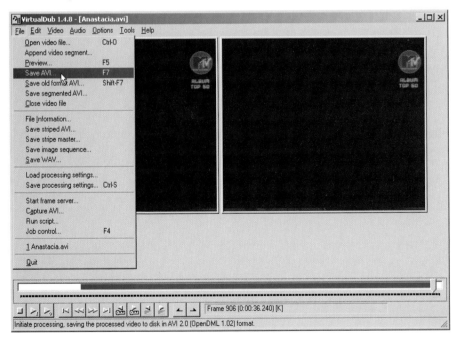

1. VirtualDub: the free capturing program

Select a name and save location for the video clip.

Click on *OK* to start the process. The encoding process begins and can be followed as long as the options *Show input video* and *Show output video*, located in the lower part of the dialog window, are enabled

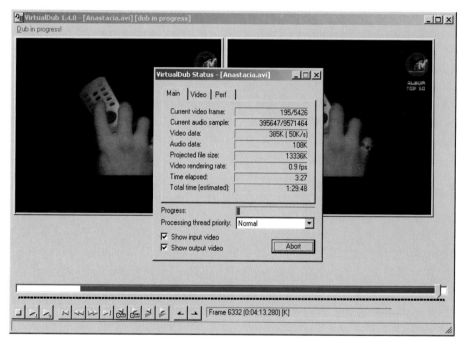

The dialog box informs you of the current video data transfer rate and the duration of the conversion process during the entire saving process.

The explorer box shows you the newly created video file compared to the original file.

The size is reduced to almost a tenth of the original.

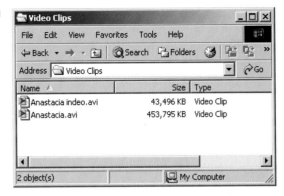

2. From video camera or video recorder to PC

If you want to use your computer not only as a high-tech video recorder but also to process your movies, then you can make good use of VirtualDub.

If your graphics card or TV card has Video-in, you can connect it to a camcorder or video recorder.

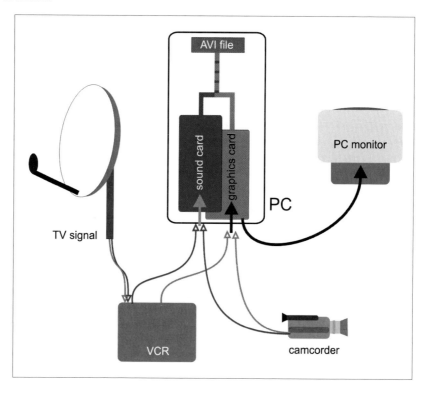

Obviously, those with a "real" video card can use the benefits of VirtualDub and need not use the capture tool supplied with the card.

The card only has to be compatible with Video for Windows.

The latest TV cards based on MPEG-2 technology, such as analog video capture cards, function using hardware compression, i.e. the video signal is digitized through the chip in the card and needs only to be saved on the hard drive.

The advantage is that compression is not dependent on computer performance, and you can capture videos even with slower systems – even in full length.

Is everything connected?

Depending on the video hardware used, there are different sockets for video and audio signals. All devices with line-out or S-video sockets such as Video-in are suitable.

Most audio line-outs are so-called Cinch sockets. If they are not there for some reason, you can always "misuse" the headphone socket as Audio-out.

With respect to the computer, you must have Video-in and Audio-in sockets available.

Some interface cards have built-in sound cards and have Video and Audio-in sockets, which is why they don't depend on external cards and don't cause compatibility problems.

There are also video cards like the DC10plus that are only concerned with the image signal. A separate sound card must be used for the audio signal.

Better cards with S-Video-in

Most recently, a PC card designed specifically for video interface offers another input, described as the S-video, Hosiden or Y/C socket:

2. From video camera or video recorder to PC

If such sockets exist (one for in and one for out), they should be used, if possible, for the quality is visibly better thanks to separate color and brightness signals.

If these components have already been mixed, as with the simple composite signal (the corresponding sockets are often indicated with Line-In/Out), the image is visibly blurred.

Obviously, this inlet must have a corresponding outlet on the player. Simple camcorders of the formats VHS-C or Video8 may not have such an S-video out, but all others have it, especially the newest digital standards miniDV or Digital8. Home video recorders have the relevant sockets mostly as S-VHS variants.

Is the image there?

If everything is connected as above, you should select the capture mode in Virtual Dub by going to *File/Capture AVI,* and display the current image, if the player is running.

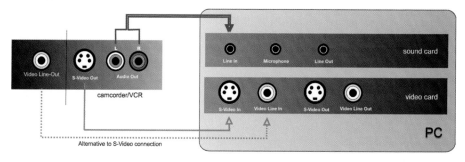

If this is not the case, then you should double-check two things:

1. Have you selected the right capture drive?

If several cards that are related to the video are installed on the system, it may be that other capturing drivers are installed as well.

In VirtualDub, it is easy to check this and to make the necessary changes.

In the capture mode, go to *Video*. The available drivers are listed.

Those activated have a dot before them.

If you want to change a driver (and the card connected to it), select the new one simply by clicking on it.

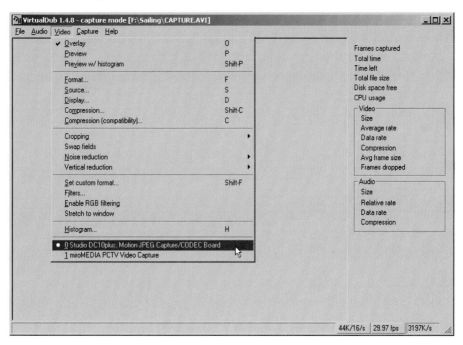

Here, a TV card is also installed in the PC, and its capture driver, *miroMEDIA PCTV Video Capture,* is enabled.

2. From video camera or video recorder to PC

2. Have you selected the correct Video-in?

Most often, a video card has two different in channels, namely the Line and S-video sockets.

If, for example, the camcorder is connected to the S-video-in of the video card, this must also be selected in the driver software of the card.

With VirtualDub, you can access the relevant driver by going to *Video/Source* in the menu.

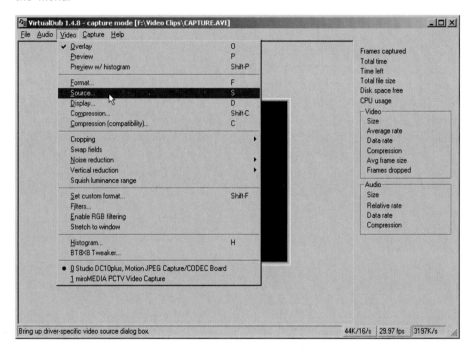

Now, call up the video card interface (it will have a different appearance from model to model and version to version).

The following image appears with DC10plus:

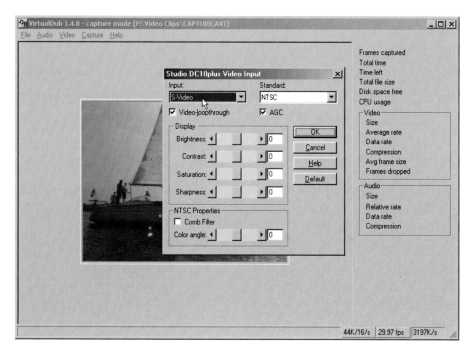

Selecting *S-Video* as the current input will make the video image appear immediately on the screen.

In addition to this function, the hardware can also influence the image quality regarding brightness, contrast, color saturation and sharpness, enabling the video to be captured as best as possible.

Selecting the interface card format

When you're choosing the format and the compression in VirtualDub, the differences between the models become evident:

For example, if you own the Pinnacle DC10plus and select the menu option *Video/ Format...*

63

2. From video camera or video recorder to PC

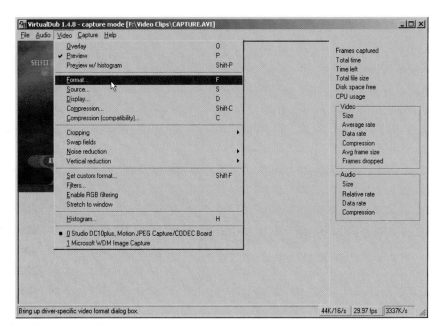

... you access directly the internal interface. Here, you can adjust all image parameters for the capture:

In the upper area, you can achieve different quality levels by combining various horizontal and vertical (here: "temporal") resolution settings. This facilitates the adaptation to the system's performance.

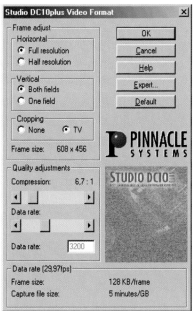

The smallest resolution is given by combining *Half Resolution* with *One field*, which corresponds to the usual quarter screen resolution for TV cards (360x270 pixels)

For maximum quality, you should record both half frames in full horizontal resolution:

If *None* is selected simultaneously under *Cropping*, the full NTSC format of 720x480 pixels can be used.

Because the full image is not displayed on the TV screen anyway, you can do away with the area that is not visible and thus save space when recording.

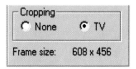

For each image format, a data transfer rate can be set with the slider:

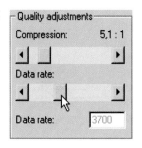

65

The higher the value selected, the less the video has to be compressed, which leads to better capturing quality. The amount of space needed does increase, however.

With this card, a special information field informs you of the amount of memory used by the current settings, which makes it possible to use the available space to the fullest.

```
┌─Data rate (29,97fps)─────────────────────────────────┐
│  Frame size:                      148 KB/frame         │
│  Capture file size:               4 minutes/GB         │
│                                                        │
└────────────────────────────────────────────────────────┘
```

Increasing the data transfer rate places high demands on the hard drive, because large amounts of data have to be written without interruption, so there are no jerks or data losses. You can determine whether the data transfer rate is realistic by using the test routine in VirtualDub, for example.

Expanding the format possibilities

In some cases, selecting a specific format can be beneficial.

If you want to create a video CD from the captured material, for example, it is best to use the CD format (352x240 pixels) or an exact multiple of it for capturing, because it ensures the best result for the subsequent MPEG encoding.

The capture board DC10plus shown here does not have these pixel ratios available. Therefore, you must set them manually:

1 Go to *Video/Set custom format.*

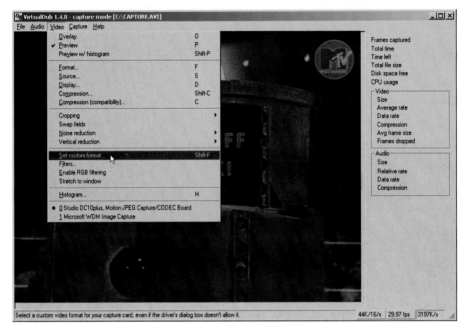

Set the dimensions for a video CD (352 x 240 pixels).

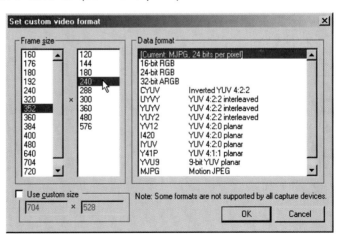

The list of different color formats on the right has little significance for most video capture cards, as they use their own formats and do not accept others.

Although selection seems possible at first, an error message appears when you start capturing:

VirtualDub capture error

Error 418: Not supported videoformat.

OK

Note

Increasing image quality
In order to increase the image quality of the video CDs you will create, you can select custom image dimensions whose one field will be captured in full resolution (e.g. 704 x 240 or 352 x 488). This theory always leads to a good compromise between image size and quality. This is especially true if the capturing process is an intermediate step to the final format, because all additional image information will lead to a better result when you convert your file to the final format.

Characteristics of capture cards

Many analog video capture cards capture in the MJPEG ("Motion **JPEG**") format and rely on a codec produced by the manufacturer and installed at the same time as the driver.

For this reason, the dialog boxes *Video/Compression...*

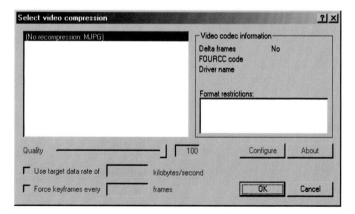

Select video compression

(No recompression: MJPG)

Video codec information

Delta frames   No
FOURCC code
Driver name

Format restrictions:

Quality   100   Configure   About

☐ Use target data rate of   kilobytes/second

☐ Force keyframes every   frames   OK   Cancel

... and *Video/Compression (compatibility)* offer no alternative compression:

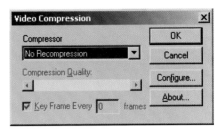

Capturing tips

When all settings have been made, you can now capture videos onto the hard drive.

Depending on your plans, following some tips can make the process easier for you.

1 If the video file is to be processed further in an editing program like MovieXone, it is advised to digitize the material block by block or scene by scene. This provides more of an overview, so that you are not searching endlessly for certain sections of a clip.

2 Create a directory for the editing project. This is briefly described below.

Now you can capture the video clip. This is described in depth starting on page **30?** and is therefore only briefly described here:

1 Start VirtualDub in the capture mode *(File/Capture AVI)*

2 Create a project directory on the hard drive (e.g. Sailing). The captured files are correspondingly placed into it with *File/Set capture file.*

3 Start the internal mode capture with *Capture/Capture video...* [F6]. Alternatively, you can use the compatibility mode by going to *Capture/Capture video (compatibility mode)* [F5].

4 Rename the file *Capture.avi* according to its content. You can now begin a new capturing process.

•

69

Using filters with the video clip

When capture is complete, you can begin editing the material with any editor, whereby VirtualDub acts only as a capture tool. But the program can do much more:

The captured video and audio files can be filtered and converted into other formats. You can optimize the video material for editing with VirtualDub as the "video processor".

Proceed in the following manner:

1 Open a clip.

2 Modify the clip by allocating filters and possibly new in and out points.

3 Export the result as a new clip.

If you were still bound to the driver and graphics/TV/video interface codecs while capturing, you can output in any file format (provided the corresponding codec is installed).

A filter interface for editing video clips is integrated into VirtualDub. With its help, you can undertake a vast number of corrections and defamiliarizations in a very simple manner.

In the following example, we will process a clip with a filter and convert it into a space-saving format.

In addition to the integrated filters, you can download others from the Internet and add them to VirtualDub. You can find a link to other filters at http://www.virtualdub.org.

Installing additional filters

Such additional filters are very small files and can be downloaded in a relatively short space of time.

In order for VirtualDub to recognize a filter the next time the program starts, you need only copy/move the file into the plug-in directory (with the extension *.vdf):

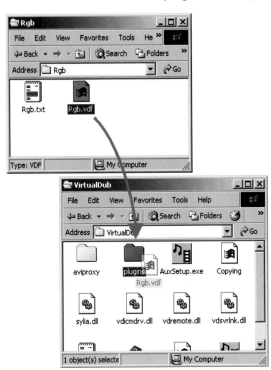

Assigning video filters

When VirtualDub is started again, you can assign one or more filters to an opened clip as follows.

By using an RGB filter you can carry out color corrections:

2. From video camera or video recorder to PC

1 Go to *Video/Filters*.

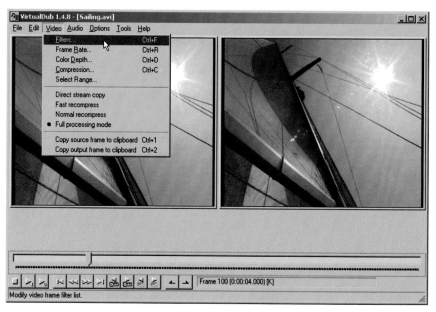

The window that appears is empty. It will later list all the filters you have used.

2 Click on the *Add* button, and all available filters are shown.

Using filters with the video clip

3 Select the filter and confirm with OK.

4 In the subsequent dialog box, click on Show Preview to check the changes directly on the video image.

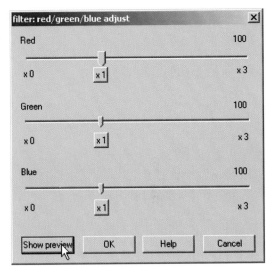

5 Now you can adjust the values for the primary colors Red, Green and Blue with the sliders.

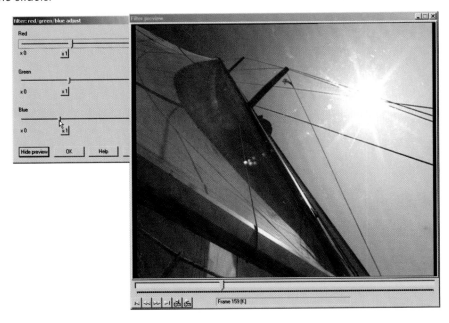

2. From video camera or video recorder to PC

6 Clicking OK takes you back to the list, to which the red/green/blue adjustment has just been added.

Any number of filters can be added in this way.

You can leave the filter menu by clicking on *OK*.

When you are in the main window again, you can assess the result in the monitor window on the right.

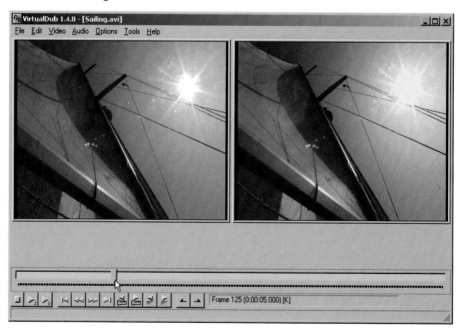

Click on the relevant *Play button* (see illustration) to run most filters in real time (even if more than one is activated):

Filter overview

VirtualDub has a lot of integrated filters.

Here are all internal filters and their functions:

Filter name	Function	Preview
2:1 reduction (high quality)	Reduces the image by halving the width and height to a quarter of the screen area.	No
3x3 average	Each pixel is made from the average of the pixels surrounding it. Causes slight blurring.	Yes
blur	Creates a slight blur that is almost imperceptible in a full picture.	No
blur more	Stronger blurring.	No
box blur	Blurring can be defined.	Yes
brightness/ contrast	Brightness and contrast control.	No
deinterlace	Joins half frames together.	No
emboss	Effect filter: image shown as relief (can be set).	No
field bob	Compensates for field jumping in field-split video by bob-deinterlacing techniques.	No
field swap	Swaps the half frame sequence.	No
fill	A rectangle can be set and filled with the desired color.	Yes
flip horizontally/ flip vertically	Flips a frame horizontally or vertically.	No
general convolution	Type of image processor that affects each pixel according to its color, as well as those surrounding it. Some values have to be entered into a matrix.	No
grayscale	Changes video clips to black and white.	No

75

2. From video camera or video recorder to PC

Filter name	Function	Preview
invert	Inverts the colors into a "negative".	No
motion blur	Creates a type of motion blur by "resonating" the previous images.	No
null transform	Copies source to destination.	No
resize	Image format can be set with pixel accuracy.	Yes
rotate	The video image can be rotated in 90° steps. Pixel measurements can be changed this way as well.	No
rotate2	Rotates the image by any angle.	Yes
sharpen	Increases the contrast of the edges to sharpen the image (can be set).	No
smoother	A dynamic soft focus that tries to retain edges and contours. Can reduce distortion.	Yes
temporal smoother	Like motion blur but constantly increasing.	Yes
threshold	Converts the image to pure black and white. The threshold can be set.	No
TV	Converts the image to NTSC.	No

Optimizing the system for capturing

Every computer is – on the basis of the endless number of possible hardware configurations during manufacturing – to some extent unique. If you aren't dealing with a specific problem which occured in a specific program, only general advice can be given, which should be heeded even more because it basically applies to every system.

There are several settings that can be made in the Windows operating system that will increase its capability during video capturing.

1. Configuring the virtual memory manually

Windows continually stores data in a virtual memory – the hard drive. The file used for this is dynamically managed, thereby regularily changing in size and costing computing time.

76

... in Windows 98

In the following input field (Windows 98) you can determine a fixed size for this file.

To have more control over this process, you can go to the *Performance* tab by going to *Start/Settings/Control Panel/System* and clicking on *Virtual Memory*.

The recommended settings were replaced here, so that Windows cannot write any swap files to the hard drives used for capturing. The maximum size (here, 512 MB) should be at least double the installed RAM.

Windows XP

In the new Windows XP, you can find such settings by going to *Start/Control Panel/System,* clicking on *Settings (Peformance)* on the *Advanced* tab and finally on the *Advanced* tab and *Change* under *Virtual Memory*.

Hard drives

Hard drives have been becoming increasingly larger and more affordable in recent years. These days, with UDMA 100 drives, you should have no trouble performing tasks at high speeds.

If you want to capture videos more frequently, you should consider installing an additional hard drive exclusively for saving video data. No operating systems of tempororary swap files should be found on such drives.

Which drive to use

As we just mentioned: IDE drives have in recent years taken a great leap forward and have in the meantime become quite suitable for video editing. There is absolutely no reason any more for using the expensive SCSI systems.

If you own a true video capture card, you should take the advice of the card's manufacturer about the approved drives and their configurations.

One piece of advice: A hard drive can never be too large, because video files can quickly consume a lot of space.

2. From video camera or video recorder to PC

Drivers

An important prerequisite is that all the latest busmaster drivers are installed, if possible. Only if the busmaster drivers function irreproachably can you ensure that the transfer of data occurs efficiently. The busmasters also ensure the smooth data transfer from the graphics/video cards to the capture location on the hard drive, and can usually be acquired from the manufacturer of the motherboard.

Enabling DMA

For optimal performance, the DMA mode has to be enabled for the hard drives.

... in Windows 98

The relevant settings can be found in the Device Manager, which you can open by going to *Start/Settings/Control Panel/System*.

Under *Disk drives* in the Device Manager, you can view the driver settings for the hard drives.

If there is no checkmark in the DMA box, you should enable it.

With older drives, the settings do not usually have the DMA enabled.

Depending on the type of hard drive, the way the settings are displayed in the Device Manger may differ. If this option doesn't exist, you can generally assume that the DMA mode has already been enabled by the drivers.

... in Windows XP/Windows 2000

The settings for the DMA were relocated somewhat in Windows XP. Although they can also be found in the Device Manger (*Start/Control Panel/System*, and *Device Manger* on the *Hardware* tab), the DMA settings can now be found under the properties for the IDE controller.

Regular defragmenting

Because of repeated deleting and writing, as time goes on, the data is fragmented more and more.

During the playback of a video stream, the reading head must as a result "jump around", which, in the worst case, can lead to a shaky playback.

The *Disk Defragmenter* tool that comes with windows rearranges the scattered file fragments, thereby once again bringing about order.

After going to *Start/Programs/Accessories/System Tools/Disk Defragmenter*, you can select a drive and, if necessary, defragment it.

It's recommended to let the program run overnight with larger hard drives, because, with the capacity of today's hard drives, the defragmentation process can easily take a couple of hours.

3. Editing videos with MovieXone

If you want to edit your digital recordings even further and insert titles, create certain transitions between individual frames, or insert/dub audio, then VirtualDub alone cannot help you and you will need an appropriate video editing program.

If you think that such a program will cost a small fortune, then you are wrong.

In addition to such price-worthy programs as DATA BECKER's "Easy Video Producer", created especially for the beginner, you can even obtain free software, such as the program MovieXone from Aist MediaLab.

MovieXone is a proper video editing program, which is similar in use to the "big" programs.

With it, you can combine clips into a movie, make small corrections to individual scenes and insert titles. You can also add a soundtrack or spoken commentary.

The finished product can be published in many ways: for instance, it can be sent out as an e-mail or burned onto a video CD.

MovieXone on the WWW

Further information about MovieXone can be obtained at www.aist.com, where you can also download the newest version of the program.

The software almost installs itself. Once you have accepted the licensing conditions, you must decide in which directory to copy the program files.

After restarting the computer, a shortcut icon for MovieXone is placed on the desktop.

MovieXone
4.0

The basic settings at program start

An editing project in MovieXone is called an "animation".

Every time you start the program, you must define the basic profile of the prospective animation.

1 In the *Schemes* tab, you will find the current settings. These can be adjusted in the neighboring tabs.

Should you change these values in any way, you can save them here as a new scheme.

2 In the *Page* tab, you can define the video page size for your project. Ideally, all clips that you want to process for your movie have the same format, i.e. they were digitalized with the same settings.

3. Editing videos with MovieXone

720x480 pixels is the typical NTSC format which is used by many analog video cards and the now widespread digital DV format.

To the right of the *Time* tab, in which you selected the video format in the beginning, there are two further tabs available, which only give you some more viewing options. For the sake of completeness, we will present them as well.

3 In the *Objects* tab, you can determine the viewing options for objects in the animation window.

Any clip or text can be an object and can be placed anywhere in the animation window.

If such an object is duplicated, you can create an offset by adjusting the numbers in the *Duplicate shift* area, so that the copy does not lie exactly on the original and can be accessed more easily. (Such duplicates cannot be created with the freeware version of MovieXone, because it supports only compositing.)

Checkmark the *Show Gadget Box* option, if you want to give the object a frame. Select the color of the frame from the *Gadget color* palette.

If an object is to move in the movie, the motion is displayed as a trajectory – provided that the *Show Trajectory* option has been activated.

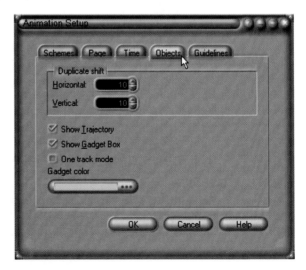

4 In the last part of the animation settings, you can define guidelines which can help with the exact positioning of the object.

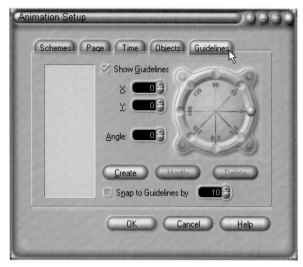

More practical guidelines can also be pulled from the rulers in the animation window at any time, however.

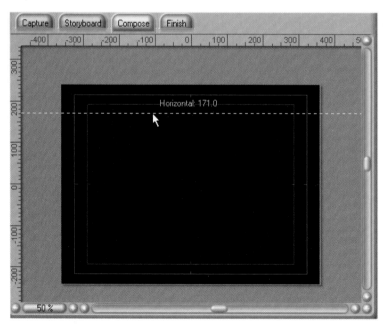

The basic structure of MovieXone

When you close the dialog box, you have adjusted all the significant settings and the basic configuration screen of MovieXone appears:

Basically, the window is split into three areas, which we will briefly introduce at this point:

1. The browser

If you want to edit a movie, you need raw material like individual video clips, graphics, sounds, but also transitions.

With the browser, you can access these individual components quickly.

This is a lot like Explorer; thus, you can access directories by double-clicking on them.

2. The timeline

The timeline is the area where the movie is created. Here, all components are brought together and placed in a chronological sequence.

The timeline, which is displayed as a kind of ruler at the top of the screen, progresses from left to right.

The video tracks run in the same direction one under the other. Underneath run the corresponding sound tracks. Image and sound are represented separately, which facilitates access to the components of a movie clip.

To view a specific part of a movie, use the so-called timeslider in the form of a blue line. You can drag the line over the timeline and drop it at the desired point.

The movie scene selected above can then be seen in the following window.

3. The preview screen

This window represents a virtual studio window and shows exactly the image selected with the timeslider. You can navigate the clip with the control buttons at the bottom.

Capturing the video material

You can't create something out of nothing, so you will first have to transfer the scenes for the planned video to the PC.

1 To do so, go to the *Capture* tab in the animation window.

2 A button allows you to determine the directory in which you want to store the captured clips. Ideally, you should switch from the default *Temp* folder in the system directory to another target directory.

It is possible to capture over a network

If you have two networked computers, you can even designate a drive on another computer as the target directory. A video stream coming in over a firewire interface at 25 Mb can easily be transferred to a second computer over a simple 100 Mb network card.

3 Click on the *Capture/Playback Hardware* button to select the desired video source (if multiple sources exist). In the example, we are working with an IEEE 1394 interface which requires the corresponding plug-in for playback.

4 Now, click on the *Capture Movie Clip* button to open the actual capture screen. Capturing over a firewire interface is as convenient as on a VCR.

To capture a scene, move to the corresponding position on the tape with the help of the controls and click on the *Play* button. To start capturing, click on the camera icon.

Always capture a little more

You shouldn't be too stingy with your hard drive space when capturing the clips and should allow an extra few seconds at the beginning and end of each in order to have enough material for eventual transitions.

6 Click again to stop the recording and to create a clip with the designation *Clip0001.avi* in the chosen target directory.

7 Record all desired scenes in the same way and then close the capture window.

Arranging clips in the right order

To create your video, you first need to arrange the clips in the right order. We will worry about the desired length of each scene only later.

As we have already mentioned, the browser in MovieXone is an interface which allows you quick access to the necessary materials.

If you have saved the digitalized video scenes in a specially created directory, you can now reap the benefits of your foresight.

3. Editing videos with MovieXone

From the browser, select the directory in which you have stored the captured video.

The actual movie is created by arranging the different video files on the timeline.

The storyboard function incorporated into MovieXone offers an easy way of arranging the files.

1 In the animation window, select the Storyboard tab.

2 Drag the different clips one after the other into the storyboard window. You can place a new scene only in the next free field.

3 Between the individual scenes, MovieXone places special fields to which you can then assign transition effects. You can change the order of the scenes at any time by dragging the scenes with the mouse. Similarly, you can insert clips between already existing scenes at a later time. The clips appear on the timeline in the same order as on the storyboard.

Trimming individual clips

Up to now, you have used the storyboard only to determine the order of the clips. Now, we will define the part of each scene we really want to use. If you only want to use a certain portion of a video file, you must set new start and end points. In the movie world, this is called trimming.

During this procedure, the clip on the hard drive is not altered. MovieXone simply "remembers" the part it is supposed to reproduce.

Trimming a video clip on the storyboard is very simple:

Double-click on a clip on the storyboard.

1 In the trimming window which opens, move the slider to the position which should be the beginning of the scene.

2 Now click on the Mark In button (open curly bracket). The blue area is shortened to illustrate the new visible area.

3 Proceed in the same manner with setting the end point of your selection.

4 To apply the changes to the storyboard, click on the Insert button.

Inserting dissolves

Until now, all clips have been connected by hard cuts by default.

Yet, with the help of the storyboard, you can also create soft transitions very easily.

1 In the browser, select the tab All Transitions, in which you will find the icon for the standard Dissolve transition.

2 Drag the icon to the field where you want to insert the transition.

3 The dissolve is inserted immediately and the timeline is updated.

4 Now, we also want to fade the sound tracks into each other. To do so elegantly, set so-called handles at the beginning and end of the overlap.

5 Drag the endpoint of Clip0004 and the starting point of Clip0005 to the very bottom of the timeline. This way, as the first clip fades out, the second fades in, which results in a soft transition for the sound.

Fade-ins and fade-outs are also possible

With *Dissolve* you can also easily create fade-ins and fade-outs. This involves fading from a scene to black (not to another clip) and vice versa.

With this technique you can start or end movies. Simply drag the dissolve icon onto the field in front of the first clip, and you have created a fade-in.

The preview area

Important: only those parts of the video for which you have set a preview area (the green bar under the time scale) can be displayed in the preview window.

The size of this area can – as with clips – be altered by dragging the margins. The area can also be shifted.

If the preview area is not available, you can create it anew by pressing the Ctrl key and clicking with the mouse.

Other interesting options

To put the scenes together into a movie, you need to place them in chronological order, as already described.

Moving clips by hand

Everywhere where there is no clip, the cursor becomes a hand with which you can shift the entire timeline horizontally while keeping the mouse button depressed. This way, you can quickly reach any position.

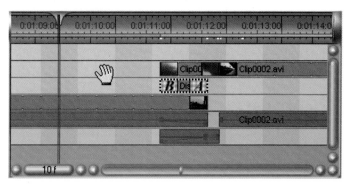

If you have already dragged scenes onto the tracks, you may find out that they need to be further shortened or elongated.

To shorten a clip located in the middle of a sequence, proceed as follows:

1 Holding down the (Alt) key simultaneously with the mouse button makes the cursor appear as shown. When this occurs, you can move the starting point of the clip to the right.

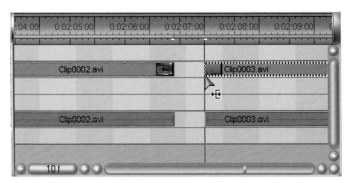

In doing so, you don't "compress" the clip and don't make it play faster - it just begins later.

2 Now all the clips that follow have to be shifted up to the altered clip.

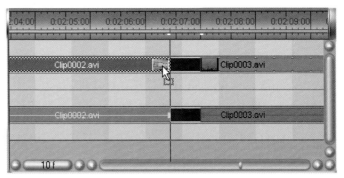

Inserting text

A real movie needs a title.

With MovieXone, you can insert a one-line text into a running image:

1 Search the browser for the *Character Generators* folder and double-click on it to open it.

2 In the folder, click on the object *Text string*.

3 Drag the icon onto the timeline.

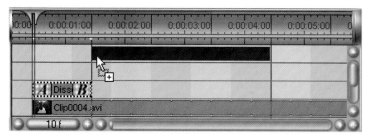

In our example, we want the movie to begin with a fade-in and the title to appear immediately behind it.

If you go with the timeslider to the text clip area, the result is immediately displayed on the preview screen.

"MovieXone" is a preset text that can be edited in the lower portion of the effect box when the text clip is active and the timeslider is located on it.

3. Editing videos with MovieXone

Scroll down the effect box window to reach the Font button and choose a different font.

The size of the title font is defined in the Compose tab in the animation window.

Rendering the finished movie

Once the work is finished and the completed movie is on the timeline, you may ask yourself what happens now.

Like VirtualDub, MovieXone can export the movie in different formats, but it can also put it out directly onto tape.

Here, too, you can achieve your goal systematically with the help of the animation window (this time, go to the *Finish* tab).

Click on the Setup button. This opens a dialog box with four tabs in which you can adjust all necessary settings.

In the Schemes tab, you can name and save the set profile, which allows you to quickly activate it for future exports in the same format.

In the following tabs you can define such a scheme very accurately.

Let us begin with the format-independent settings, like the *Render Range one.*

You can render either the whole movie (*All*) or only a section of it (*Range*). The values in *From* and *To* correspond to the range defined in the timeline and indicated by a red line above the time scale.

To define the range, click with your mouse while holding down the Ctrl key. You can then extend or shift it like a clip.

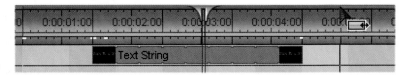

In the *Renderer* tab, you can select the internal renderer and the quality level.

The decisive settings for the rendering can be adjusted in the *Format* tab.

3. Editing videos with MovieXone

Depending on your purpose, different formats can be selected:

- Digital video formats

- MovieXone supports direct video import and export for digital video formats like miniDV or Digital8, as long as the PC has an appropriate interface, usually an expansion card.

- Such cards have several designations, but they mean the same thing: IEEE-1394, Firewire or i-Link from Sony all stand for a small connection which enables the simultaneous transfer of image and sound data from the camcorder to the computer hard drives over a single cable. If the camcorder has another DV-in, it can even be used as a recorder for the finished movie.

- If you want to export in such a format, select *Digital Video (AVI)*.

- Analog formats of TV/video cards for transfer to video tape

- If you have digitized analog sources with a TV or video card (either via Virtual Dub, MovieXone or the recording software in the video card), it is advised to save the finished movie in the same format as the original clips and play it back with the video card software in order to record it onto video over the analog outlets.

- Here, the individual clips were digitized with the MJPEG codec of DC10plus.

- To launch the codecs installed in Windows, first select *Microsoft Video (AVI)*.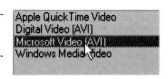

- The image size should be that of the original material – here 720 x 480.

- With *Compression Options* you can select the codec.

• Under *Compressor*, you can select the video card codec from the pull-down menu.

• Depending on the codec, this dialog box has different parameter settings (here, for instance, the compression quality can be set with a slider).
• All other settings should be left as they are.

Exporting for video CD

In order for the movie to be burned onto a CD and be played back by a DVD player, it must be converted to the MPEG-1 or MPEG-2format, which is not possible in MovieXone but only with a special encoder program like TMPEGEnc.

As before, the same codec used for capturing the clip must be used to export it in order to avoid data loss. The higher the quality of the original material in TMPEGEnc, the better the MPEG files will be.

The actual rendering process

If all format settings have been adjusted, you can close the dialog box and return to the animation window.

Click on Render to open a file selection dialog box where you can determine the target path.

3. Editing videos with MovieXone

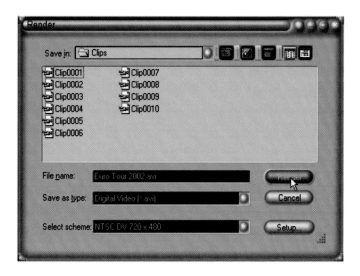

Once the name of the movie file is entered, you can start the rendering process by clicking on *Render.*

You can follow the entire procedure in a special window.

4. Post-editing the video

It is not always possible to capture videos perfectly. Reception related image noise can already make a noticeable difference in the quality of the video CD to be created. And there is one more annoyance: the permanently visible station logos.

To a certain extent, such problems can be solved with VirtualDub, or, more precisely, with the available filters.

Improving the quality of images containing noise

The foremost thing that makes life difficult when compressing video clips is image noise. There are several possible causes of this:

- TV reception is not optimal
- faulty connections
- interfering signals (e.g. from a computer, cell phone, etc.)

Such noise leads every codec to interpret it as complex image information. Compression of the images can become substantially worse – the result is a dramatic decrease in the quality of the resulting AVI file or MPEG stream.

In many cases, the result can be noticeably improved by smoothing the image with the help of a softening tool.

1 Load the clip to be edited by going to *File/Open video file...*

2 Select the desired audio and video codecs.

3 Then click on *Video/Filters...*

4 In the window that opens, click on *Add...* to add a filter.

5 From the list, select the filter *blur more* and leave the window by clicking on *OK*.

4. Post-editing the video

6 Back in the main window, you can see the results immediately by moving back and forth within the clip.

7 The clip can now be saved in the filtered version by going to *Save as AVI*.

Instead of using *blur more*, you can also use the *smoother* filter; it provides good results because it only tries to smooth surfaces. It uses a preview which you can use to refine all the settings.

If you are unsure, test both filters using a small video clip.

Removing station logos

Every television station includes a permanantly displayed logo in one of the corners of the image in order to make itself recognizable when zapping through the tons of available channels.

Such an image can be bothersome in many cases – so why not get rid of it? The corresponding VirtualDub filter makes it no problem.

You won't be able to find the necessary filter among the ones included with the program. Here, it helps to use the Internet. By going to VirtualDub's homepage, www.virtualdub.org , you will also have access to filters by other programmers.

We will use the *logoaway* filter created by Krzysztof Wojdon.

1 Load the video clip that needs to be cleaned up into VirtualDub (*File/Open video fil ...*).

2 Determine the output codes for the image and sound.

3 Now click on *Video/Filters...*, and, in the window that appears, click on *Add...*, so that you finally end up in the *Add Filter dialog* window. If logoaway was installed correctly using the *Load...* button, it will appear in the list of available filters, where it can be selected.

4 Confirmining it by clicking on *OK* will open the *logoaway* dialog window.

5 Click on the *Show preview* button in order to display the video to be edited, and use the slider to select an image in which the logo is nicely visible.

6 In the dialog window, enable the option *Visible borders* in order to see the region to be manipulated – indicated by the dashed rectangle – in the preview window.

7 The position and size of the selection can be set to the exact pixel with the values *Logo border position* and/or *Logo border size*.

8 Once you have set all the parameters, don't forget to disable *Visible borders* again; otherwise, the borders will be visible in the video.

9 Finally, close all the dialog windows with *OK* and allow the film to be newly computed by going to *File/Save as AVI*.

Using this method, quite acceptable results can be obtained by "smearing" the pixels in the surrounding area. The flatter the image, the better the result will be.

Removing commercials

Who's not familiar with it: just when the movie is getting exciting ... a commercial break!!

If you want to record a movie on video without such disruptions, you need to keep VCR's remote in your hand, stop the tape during a commercial break, rewind it a bit, and, with the image paused, wait for the next part of the movie.

In contrast, you can use the computer and, without any stress, remove the annoying commercial breaks at their exact position after the taping.

This can be done with VirtualDub in the following way:

1 Load the movie file by going to *File/Open video file...*

2 Use the slider to go to the beginning of the first commercial break. (With the help of the double-arrow forward and rewind keys, you can even move frame by frame.)

3 Once you've reached the first frame of the region to be deleted, click on the *Mark in* button.

4 Now, to define the end of the commercial break: move to the last frame of the break and indicate it with the Mark out button as the end point of the selection region.

5 The region you have selected in this way can be deleted by going to the menu item *Edit/Delete Frames* or by pressing the [Delete] key.

6 Repeat steps 2-5 for all undesireable interruptions and save the entire movie by going to *Save as AVI*.

Creating a movie clip from segments

What's even simpler than deleting sections in a video is combining several smaller AVI files into a larger clip.

1 In VirtualDub, open the first section of the clip (e.g. *Clip001.avi*).

2 Afterwards, you can use the *File/Append AVI segment...* command to add all of the remaining sections in chronological order.

3 And, as the very last thing, save the combined movie by going to *File/Save as AVI...*

5. From DVD to PC

If you have ever tried to copy a DVD movie file from your DVD-Rom onto your hard drive, you will have probably encountered the following message:

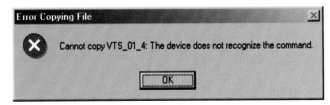

The reason for this is that DVDs are usually copy protected to prevent such copying.

Because copy protections are created by mere humans, it was only a matter of time until someone found a way around this one, and so, a "remedy" was born in Norway in the form of a small program.

The software named DeCSS ("De-Content Scrambling System") cracks the DVD encryption and facilitates copying files onto the hard drive. The first versions of DeCSS were difficult to use, but more convenient versions have since appeared to facilitate such copying.

Caution when ripping DVDs

This process – known as "ripping" – is completely prohibited and thus illegal unless the DVDs belong to you, or unless you have obtained express permission to make a copy.

Once the ripped files are on your hard drive, you can convert them to video CD or Super video CD format and burn them onto normal CDs.

This method has a crucial disadvantage: for each DVD, you need a few gigabytes of free space on your hard drive.

The more sophisticated alternative is to use a small freeware tool which reads in the data from the DVD and converts it directly, so you only need to have free space for the later (S) video CD(s).

All-in-one: DVDx

Not long ago, you still needed separate programs for ripping and encoding. In the meantime, however, you can find software solutions which put everything into one package.

DVDx is an easy-to-use program, in addition to which it is also free. As far as the hardware is concerned, you still need a DVD drive, for a CD-ROM drive can't read DVDs.

More on DVDx

At http://www2.labdv.com/dvdx, you will find an extensive forum in which users share their experiences, in addition to the most current version of the program.

Installation is no problem

DVDx is one of those programs for which you don't have to go through a setup. The advantage: no drivers or other files which could endanger your system are installed inconspicuously.

Simply put all your DVDx files into a directory of your choice and start *DVDx.exe*.

Collecting trailers on CD with DVDx

Many DVDs contain trailers (which appear in cinemas before a movie is released) in addition to the main feature.

These trailers are spread over many of your DVDs, and it would be great to put them onto one CD to enjoy them in sequence.

The legal consequences must be stressed again: in essence, you will be making pirated copies of these trailers, which is punishable by law.

The import settings in DVDx

With DVDx, you can target a specific trailer and convert it to the MPEG format necessary for a VCD or SVCD.

It is very helpful to have watched the DVD beforehand, in order to know about how long the trailer is (in our case, about 2 minutes 45 seconds). This way, it is a lot easier to find the title in DVDx afterwards.

1 Insert the desired DVD into the drive and start a software DVD player (like WinDVD) to share the drive. This way, you avoid any DVDx reading error messages.

2 Start DVDx and select *File/Open DVD root*.

3 The selection dialog box which opens displays all available titles. (Don't confuse this which the actual items that can be played. This has more to do with the way the DVD is structured.)

Because the length of *Title01* corresponds to the length of the main movie, the trailer must be hiding under *Title02*. Click on the latter, then confirm your choice by clicking on *Select*.

4 A window opens, in which you can set the parameters for reading in the data. In the *Program Chain* area, you can view the available movies for this title in the *Index* listbox, where you can also select them individually. If you know the length of the trailer you are looking for, you will now be rewarded.

5 In the *Audio* area, you can select the desired sound track from the ones at your disposal. On the DVD in our example, there are two English sound tracks (one for 6-channel Dolby Surround and one for "normal" stereo installations).

In either case, the final product will be a simple stereo sound track. To obtain a balanced mixing ratio when you mix Dolby Surround down to stereo, you should enable the Dolby Surround checkbox.

6 In the *Subtitle* field, you can use the listbox to decide whether you want to show or hide subtitles.

7 The field *Misc* contains the *iDCT* listbox, in which you can select the rendering technique for the image conversion. The *FPU* option delivers the best results and takes about 15% more time.

8 The category *Save your DVD Drive* is especially useful. Here, you can make a certain amount of storage space available for the software, so you don't have to continually access the DVD-ROM drive. This is an excellent feature for reading directly from DVDs.

Clicking on *OK* will take you to the main window of the program.

The export settings in DVDx

The main window is dominated by the preview window. Move the slider located underneath to make sure you have selected the right movie.

If you have selected the wrong movie by mistake, it isn't too late to make changes. You can return to the previous dialog window at any time by going to *Settings/Input settings*.

In our example, you can see that the image was stretched horizontally. Now, you need to adjust the export settings (*Settings/Output settings*). The following are the most important parameters:

1 The very first thing you need to do is to determine the output format: *video CD* (*MPEG1*), *Super Video (MPEG2)* or *AVI output*. The relevant settings are automatically loaded for the two MPEG formats. In our example, we want to create a video CD.

2 Under *Export Settings*, you can set the *Resolution* (here, *352x240* pixels, the resolution for a video CD). In addition, you can also set the picture zoom. For a full picture, select the *Full* option from the *Zoom* listbox. This immediately eliminates the distortion in the main window.

3 Not far beneath, you will find a number box labeled *Max Frame*. Here, you can manually enter the number of frames you want to convert. Usually, you want all frames to be converted, so you only need to click on *Whole*. DVDx then determines the number of frames and can thus estimate the necessary computation for the encoding more exactly.

4 It is important for the computation that you select the correct type of processor: if you are an Intel fan, leave the default *MMX*; if you are an Athlon user, switch over to *MMX + 3DNow*.

5 If you want to convert a longer movie, you can even enter the length of your blank CDs. This saves the tedious splitting of the MPEG file. In our example, we are only producing a short movie, so the setting is unimportant in this case.

Click on *Apply* to retain the selected settings and to return to the main window.

Determining the output path and starting the encoding

Now, you only need to decide where you want to save the converted movie.

If you have been scrolling through the movie file, don't forget to move the slider back to the beginning, for it determines the starting position for the render range.

1 Click on the *Select Output* button.

2 In the following window, click on *Browse*.

3 In the file selection dialog window, select the directory and file name.

4 Back in the main window, click on *Encode* to start the conversion.

5. From DVD to PC

DVDx keeps you up-to-date on the conversion process.

From the resulting MPEG file, you can now burn a video CD with a burning program like Roxio's Easy CD Creator.

6. Smart Ripper and FlasK: Manual alternatives to DVDx

DVDx has very good handling and makes further programs – with the exception of burning software – practically superfluous.

Still, we would like to quickly mention some alternatives which, until not long ago, were almost indispensible when it came to ripping or converting DVD content. In addition, these alternatives are somewhat more flexible.

Copying the movie files to the hard drive

With SmartRipper, you can target the desired trailer and copy it to the directory of your choice on your PC.

 SmartRipper on the WWW?
We cannot legally provide you with the official downloading address for SmartRipper. However, you should be able to easily find it using any search engine.

1 Place the DVD in the drive and start your DVD player software, such as Power DVD.

2 If the DVD is recognized and played back, you can close the player and launch SmartRipper. With many films, this process makes it possible to decrypt the data and helps if the ripping procedure does not start.

3 After the DVD is read and analyzed, the main window of the program opens where you can select the movie you want to copy under *Title-/Program Chain-/ Angle*.

4 Before the DVD data is read in, you must determine where you want to save the future file. Click on the folder icon to select a directory of your choice.

6. Smart Ripper and FlasK: Manual alternatives to DVDx

The information next to the target path gives you the amount of hard drive space at your disposal:

5 Click on *Start* to begin the reading process.

After the ripping is completed, you can find the files on the hard drive:

Converting DVD data with FlasK

Now we need to switch software, for this is pretty much the end of SmartRipper's capabilities.

The DVD files saved on the hard drive only need to be converted to video CD format.

A classic program for this purpose is FlasK, which, like VirtualDub, is small and simple and available as freeware.

Different versions of FlasK

As with any other software, FlasK is also constantly being updated, and there are several versions of the program.

The very popular FlasKMPEG 0.594 version has been in circulation for some time.

Its successor, FlasKMPEG 0.6, is still in the starting blocks. One (current) significant difference between the two versions is that FlasK 0.6 (shown here) will only accept VOB files, whereas FlasK 0.594 can also open IFO files.

The maximum size for a VOB file on a DVD is 1024 MB, thus a movie has to be divided into several VOB files. In plain terms, an IFO file is a list of the VOB files needed to play back a movie.

Thus, FlasK 0.594 can open entire movies and convert them in one go, while, in version 0.6, you must convert VOB by VOB and then assemble the individual sections using another program. In the case of MPEG clips for a (S)VCD, the MPEG tools in TMPEGEnc offer this useful function.

FlasK on the WWW

At the following address, you can find the most current version of FlasK, as well as further information about the program:

http://www.flaskmpeg.net

Trailers, on the other hand, always fit into a single VOB file and can be processed with version 0.6 and the advantages associated with it.

Processing individual VOB files with FlasK 0.6

When you start the program for the first time, you first need to select the language, after which the start screen resembling a media player appears.

1 Go to *File/Open Media*.

The current version of FlasK is not suitable for processing AVIs and can only use MPEG files as original material.

6. Smart Ripper and FlasK: Manual alternatives to DVDx

2 Select the VOB file you want to convert.

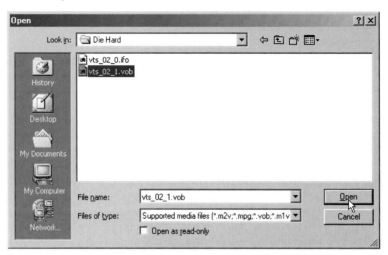

3 The editing window appears, in which you can adjust all relevant settings.

The conversion of the VOB file proceeds as follows:

Coonfiguring the output

Two important settings which are required for achieving a standard format are those for the picture size and the sampling frequency for the sound. Adjusting these settings is very easy in this case.

To do so, click on *Configure.*

The window *FlasK MPEG Options* facilitates the adjustment of these settings.

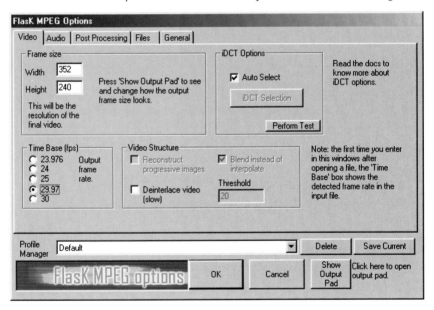

In the lower part of the window, you can see the *Profile Manager,* where you only have to select the desired profile (here, we want to burn the trailer to a video CD).

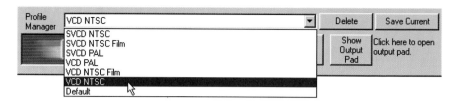

Afterwards, you can already leave the options window by clicking on OK.

Selecting the encoder

Thus far, only the outer elements of the future video have been determined: frame size, frame rate, etc.

The decisive values, however, are the internal ones:

Back in the *Control Panel,* the next step is to select the output format.

The video stream for a video CD must be in MPEG-1 format. To create such a video file, you need a so-called encoder. For FlasK, there is the free encoder bbMPEG available with which you can create MPEG-1 videos.

To render with bbMPEG, click on the *Select Output* button.

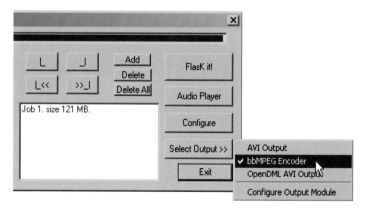

In contrast to other formats, the encoder bbMPEG is not configured by selecting the command *Configure Output Module* in the same menu, but only once the conversion has started.

Confirm your selection by clicking on *OK*. You can now exit the window and return to the *Control Panel*.

After all necessary settings have been made, you only need to begin the conversion.

Click on *FlasK it!* to start the show.

The window of bbMPEG opens. Click on the *Settings* button to configure the encoder.

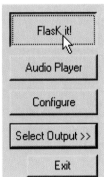

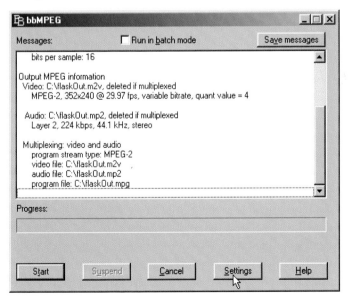

6. Smart Ripper and FlasK: Manual alternatives to DVDx

To create a video CD profile, you need to adjust a few settings in three of the tabs.

1 In the *General Settings* tab, you should keep the checkmarks in the *Encoding* and *Multiplexing* fields. They ensure that both the video and the audio tracks are converted to MPEG format and are then converged in a video stream (multiplexed).

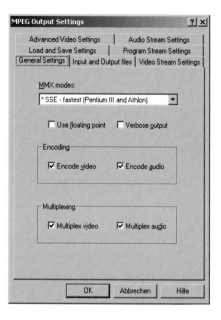

2 In the *Video Stream Settings* tab, click on *VideoCD* under *Video type* to enable the creation of a video stream in video CD format.

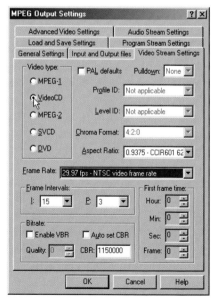

3 In the *Input and Output files* tab, enter the location and name of the target file; you can ignore the rest of the settings.

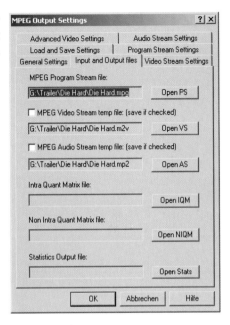

4 Once you have adjusted the settings, you can save them under a distinguishing name by clicking on the *Save Settings* button.

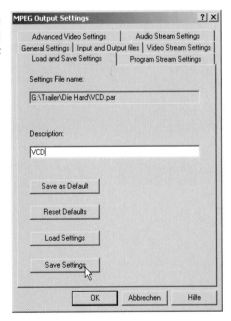

6. Smart Ripper and FlasK: Manual alternatives to DVDx

5 Click on *OK* to exit the dialog window and then on *Start* to launch the conversion process.

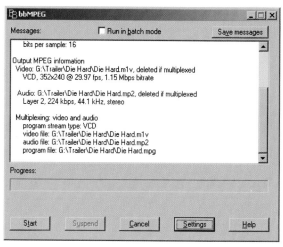

During conversion, the frame currently being processed is shown in a preview window.

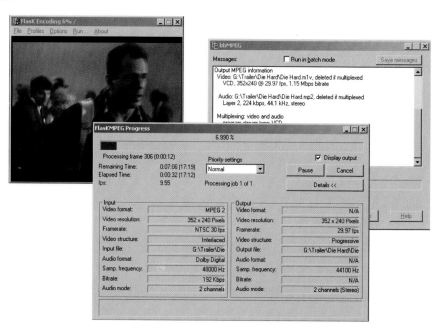

You can disable this display if you would rather do without it.

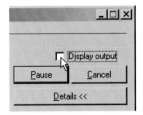

This saves valuable computing time (approximately 15%), which is noticeable right away and can save hours with long movies.

After the MPEG file is converted (with a 1200-MHz Athlon processor, this will take about 8 minutes for every 3½minutes of material), bbMPEG encodes the sound and then mixes (multiplexes) the video and audio streams together into a so-called program stream.

The resulting MPEG file can now be burned as a video CD together with other files (see chapter "Burning onto CD").

7. Creating video CD material from movie files

Capture programs like VirtualDub or the capture tools supplied with video cards usually facilitate creating AVI files based on the most diverse codecs.

As all types of video CD require MPEG coded video streams, you have to encode the video files, for which you need a suitable MPEG encoder.

A stand-alone application opens a movie file, as in VirtualDub, and then encodes it into the MPEG format.

In addition to many (rather expensive) commercial MPEG encoders, there is the software TMPGEnc which is available as freeware and which has more features than most other products.

Thanks to its compact size, TMPGEnc can be downloaded very quickly from its homepage.

TMPGEnc on the WWW

At the following address, you will find the most current version of the program, as well as additional information about TMPGEnc:

http://www.tmpgenc.com

The settings before starting with TMPGEnc

In the following example, we will be converting a short movie file (the Euro Tour movie created with MovieXone in chapter 4) into the MPEG format for a video CD.

After the program start, TMPGEnc appears like this:

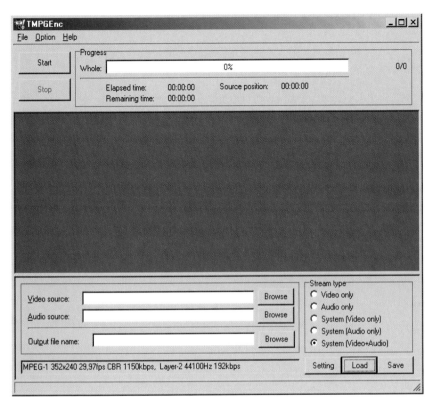

This is how you prepare for the encoding process:

1 In the lower half of the screen, search for the clip from which the MPEG video stream will be created by clicking on *Browse*.

7. Creating video CD material from movie files

2 Here we will select the short Euro Tour movie created in MovieXone.

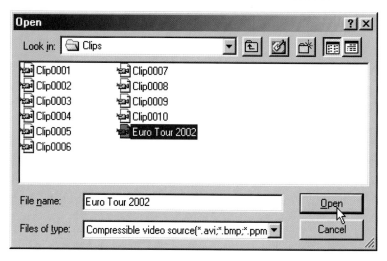

3 In TMPEGEnc, the clip appears automatically under both *Video* and *Audio source* because the file contains both image and sound data.

If the encoded movie was created with separate sound and video files, these can also be selected separately under *Video source* and *Audio source*.

Under *Output file name*, TMPGEnc automatically enters the directory of the original clip as the target directory for the MPEG file.

Use different hard drives

With longer projects, it is advised to place the original and target files on separate drives. This way, the reading and writing heads on the drives don't have to jump back and forth all the time, which shortens the encoding process and protects the hard drive.

4 Now decide whether a VCD or SVCD is to be created and select the required profile. This is no problem as TMPEGEnc is supplied with the most important settings by default.

Click on *Load* to load the desired profile.

If all TMPEGEnc files were copied to the same directory, you will get directly to the *Template* folder where you can find the individual profiles.

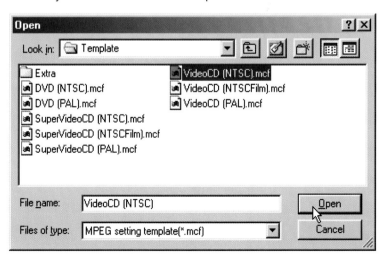

7. Creating video CD material from movie files

For this example, we want to create a video CD. Because the TV standard in the US is NTSC, you must select the corresponding NTSC profile.

After making the selection, the settings details are displayed in the lower part of TMPEGEnc's main window.

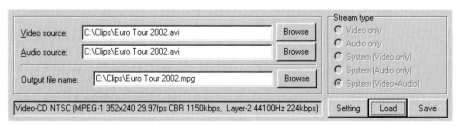

The following can be derived from the display:

1. The data stream created will correspond to the MPEG-1 format.

2. The frame dimensions are 352x240 pixels.

3. CBR stands for Constant Bit Rate and means that a constant bit rate is used here. Thus, every second of film necessitates the same amount of data, namely 1150 kpbs (the number following CBR).

4. The sound will be compressed with a sampling frequency of 44100 Hz and a data transfer rate of 224 kbps to MPEG-1, Layer-2. (A layer is a level of compression; here, the second level is used.)

Now we can create the MPEG file.

Converting to the right format

Click on the *Start* button to begin the encoding.

The default settings of TMPEGEnc ensure that the encoding process can be followed on a preview screen.

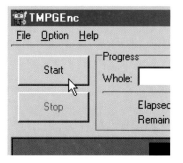

7. Creating video CD material from movie files

Similarly, the *Elapsed time*, the *Remaining time*, and the current position within the movie clip (*Source position*) are constantly displayed in the upper portion of the window.

After encoding, the MPEG clip can be found in the destination directory and can usually be played back with Windows' Media Player. To create a CD from the movie, you will need a burner that supports this format, e.g. Easy CD Creator from Roxio.

8. Compatibility with CD capacity

A standard blank CD has a capacity of up to 700 MB, which seems pretty low compared to the capacity of a movie DVD which can be up to 9 GB.

Consequently, the maximum playback time of a video CD is 80 minutes, and a SVCD will reach its limit after approximately 40 minutes.

You can easily reach file sizes of 1 GB or higher if, for instance, you save a whole movie on your hard drive using VirtualDub and then convert it to MPEG-1 format using TMPEGEnc in order to create a video CD.

The movie has to be split up between two or more CDs and the MPEG file cut accordingly.

The freeware encoder TMPEGEnc once again proves its versatility when post-editing MPEG files.

The Merge & Cut options

This inconspicuous tool is actually a small editing program which offers quite a few editing options:

1. Cutting out an area
If you are loading only one clip, you can save a cut version by defining a new start and end position. This is ideal if, for instance, you want to get rid of credits or simply want to divide a movie into several sections.

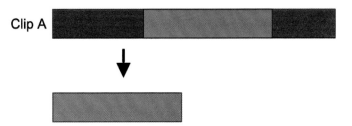

Clip A

8. Compatibility with CD capacity

2. Merging several movie clip sections to create a new clip
If you load the same clip several times, a new movie can be created from different sections. This is a good way to remove advertisements.

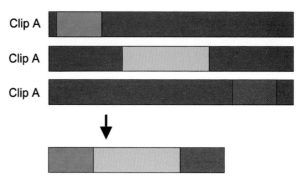

3. Merging individual clips
A new movie clip can either be made from a number of small clips or, if desired, from sections of individual clips.

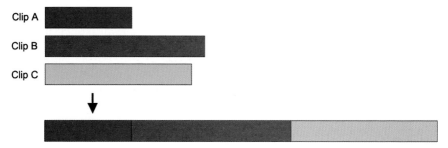

A large movie clip is cut

Large movie clips in MPEG-1 format as well as in MPEG-2 format used for SVCDs can be easily cut with the Merge & Cut tool. The resulting smaller movie clips will then conveniently fit onto two or more CDs.

The term "cut" is actually not accurate as, in reality, two entirely new clips are produced. Consequently, there always has to be adequate space on the hard drive of your computer.

The movie used in this example was created as a VCD movie and has a length of 1 hour 31 mins and 35 secs; therefore, two blank CDs are necessary to save it in its entirety.

1 Start TMPGEnc and go to *File/MPEG Tools.*

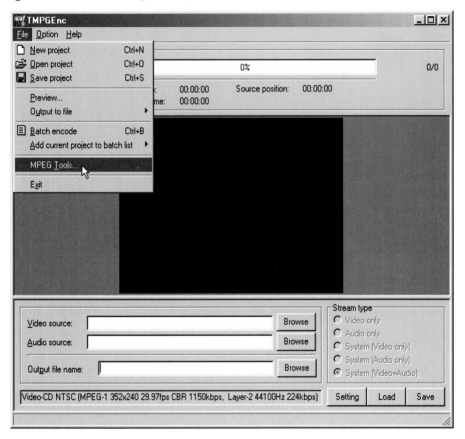

8. Compatibility with CD capacity

2 From the dialog window that opens, select the *Merge & Cut* tab.

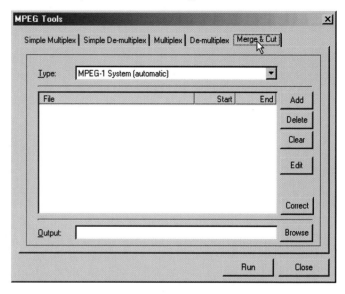

3 Select the format of the clip (i.e. *MPEG-1 Video-CD*) from the *Type* listbox.

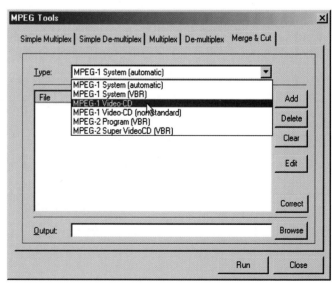

This information is necessary to create clips that will conform to the chosen format. Especially MPEG movies cannot be easily cut at any position, as they consist of entire index frames as well as B and P frames, which are derivatives of previous index frames.

4 Click on *Add* to open the MPEG movie to be cut.

The movie you select in the dialog box will appear in the file list below.

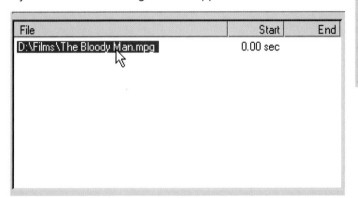

File	Start	End
D:\Films\The Bloody Man.mpg	0.00 sec	

Add

Delete

Clear

Edit

5 Double-click this entry to open a window in which you can edit the clip.

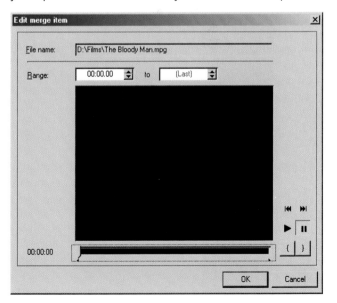

Edit merge item

File name: D:\Films\The Bloody Man.mpg

Range: 00:00.00 to (Last)

00:00:00

OK   Cancel

8. Compatibility with CD capacity

Set a new start and end position for the clip.

The clip is cut as follows: First, select the section which will be saved on the first CD. The start of the movie remains the same; only the end of the new movie file has to be set.

Use the slider and the buttons to the right of it to navigate through the movie.

Above the *Play* and *Pause* buttons, you will find two buttons with which you can go back or forward in the clip, frame by frame.

If you want to obtain two CDs of about the same size, set the end position of the first part of the movie in the middle of the movie.

If, on the other hand, you want to fill the first CD to capacity (for instance, if you want to add data to the second CD), the end position should be set after 74 or 80 minutes (depending on the size of the blank CD).

For this example, the movie was cut in half. By looking at the movie frame by frame in the editor, you can locate the last frame of the last scene very precisely; however, the final result won't be cut as precisely, due to the restrictions of the MPEG format.

Click the end position selection button (bracket symbol) at the lower right to save the position. The selected area appears black in the slider panel.

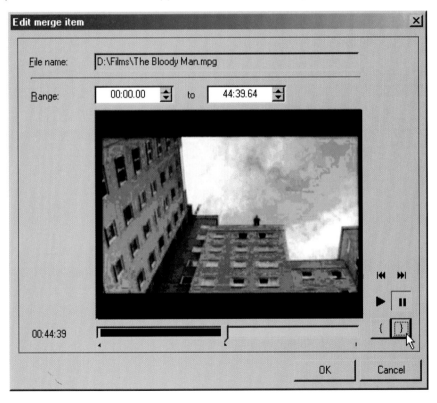

8. Compatibility with CD capacity

You can close the window by clicking on *OK*. In the clip list, the new end of the clip is displayed as a numerical value (in seconds).

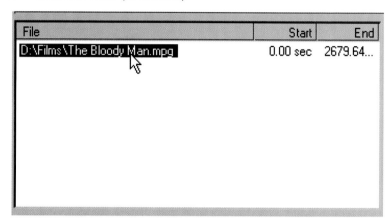

In the *Output* text box at the bottom, assign a name to the first part of the movie and use the *Browse* button to select the corresponding directory, ...

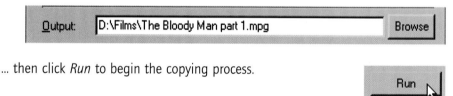

... then click *Run* to begin the copying process.

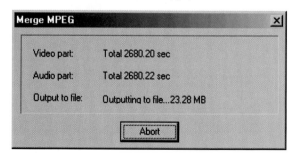

TMPEGEnc keeps you posted of the current status of the copy process.

After the new file has been created, you will find yourself back in the previous dialog box.

Now, we want to copy the second part of the movie to another file:

1 Double-click the same clip to open it again.

The values set before are still available and very useful for setting a new start position.

2 Set the slider to the previous End position.

It is very useful to alternately click on the Mark-In (open bracket) and frame-by-frame buttons to display the exact numeric position in the left *Range* box.

8. Compatibility with CD capacity

3 The end position, on the other hand, is set very quickly: simply move the slider all the way to the right and click the *End position* button.

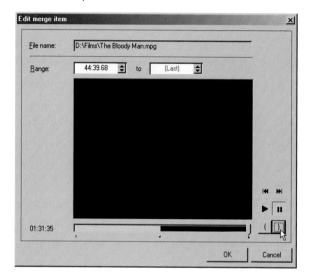

In the second *Range* box, the term *Last* should appear, which assures you that the clip has been selected up to the last frame.

4 Now you only need to select the target directory and name for the second half of the movie under *Output*.

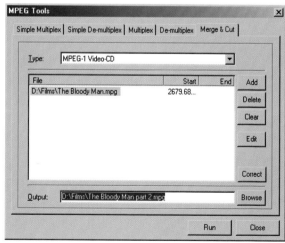

5 After both halves have been created successfully, the original file can be deleted.

It is also possible to make one movie clip from several small ones

This tool can be used for more than just cutting movie clips.

It can also be used to merge different small movies (or movie sections) to one big MPEG file, provided that all movie files are of the same type.

In this case, all you have to do is to click the *Add* button to add further clips.

9. Burning onto CDs

The results of all your efforts should not remain forever on your computer's hard drive and should therefore be finally saved on conventional CDs.

Until recently, burning video CDs was an exotic feature that was only offered by some very expensive authoring programs, such as "Videopack".

In the meantime, every decent burning program can handle creating VCDs.

Using software taken from Adaptec's "CD Creator", Roxio has developed a product for the consumer market which makes creating CD projects easier through a series of Wizards.

In the following, we will briefly illustrate how to use this program to create standard video CDs.

Video CDs with a menu

You can use Roxio's CD Creator to also create simple menu structures which are supported by DVD players and can be navigated remotely. You can find more detailed information about this in the "From VHS ToDVD", part of the DATA BECKER line of books.

Video CDs can be used for more than just saving movies

VCDs are so-called bridge discs , which consist of an actual video CD part and an ISO part – a data region that can be read by the computer. Therefore, remaining space can be used for saving "normal" data, such as documents or the relevant websites for the movie, as well as software or graphics.

Starting with the Wizard

If the program was installed, it can be started by using the shortcut on the desktop, or by going to the so-called *Project Selector* (right-click on the desktop icon):

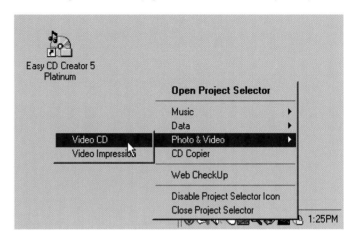

Those who prefer something more visually engaging can choose the latter way and select the appropriate project; in our case, *Video CD*.

Regardless of what decision you make, the CD Creator Wizard will load in order to make your life easier.

Unlike with most Wizards, the user will be guided through each of the steps involved in creating a CD in a clear and understandable way. Each newly created project can still be subsequently altered.

The very first thing you must do is to decide on the type of CD.

For our illustration, we simply want to burn a movie to disc. Therefore, select the option *Simple Video Sequence*:

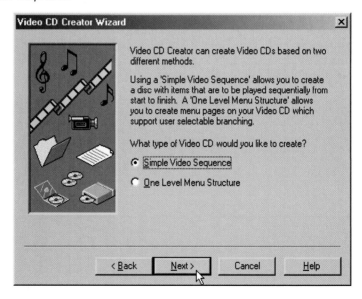

Selecting the film files

The next dialog box allows you to select the film files.

1 You must have at least one film, which requires clicking the *Add...* button at least once:

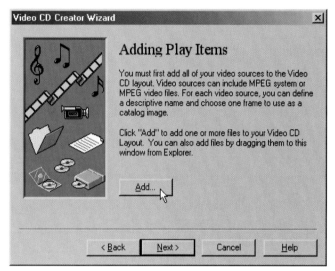

2 Select the desired MPEG file through the file selection dialog box.

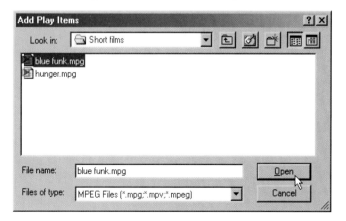

9. Burning onto CDs

3 A window for the selected film opens, in which the properties for that clip can be controlled.

The *General* tab provides information regarding the existence of sound and picture. The scrollbar underneath the picture window can be used to move throughout the film to check its contents.

In addition to the file path, the basic film parameters such as format, picture size and length are shown In the *Video* tab.

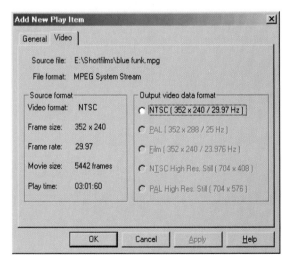

Go through steps 1 to 3 for each additional film to be added. Once you have finished adding the clip(s), proceed by clicking on *Next*:

Now the start sequence has to be determined. In our example, this is the actual movie itself.

4 All the play items loaded up to this point are shown in the left window. We only want the first movie, so we click on the *Add...* button once.

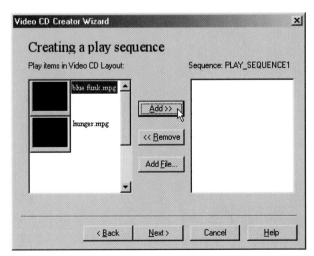

9. Burning onto CDs

The selected film then appears in the right window as the start sequence. This section is completed by clicking on *Next*.

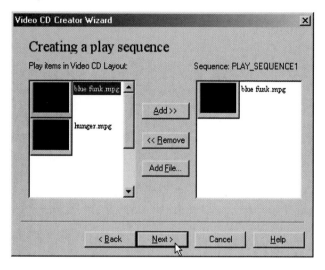

Once all the play sequences have been determined, the work can be viewed with the internal player.

Clicking on *Playback* will start a type of video CD simulation.

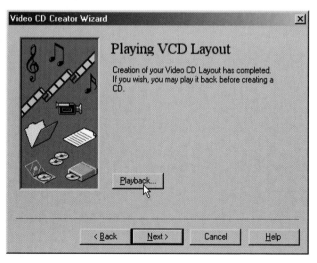

The playback feature is useful for ensuring you have selected the correct clip before actually burning in onto CD

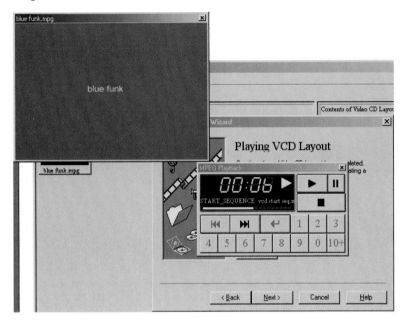

If the virtual CD has passed the test, the last step involved is to close the playback, click on *Next*, select *Create the CD now* and click on *Finish*.

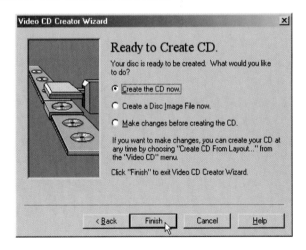

9. Burning onto CDs

The necessary file(s) will be assembled immediately, and the burner will kick into action. Now pat yourself on the back for a job well done.

Index

Index

Index

Notes

Notes

Notes

Notes